VOICES
ON
CHOICE

The Education Reform Debate

CONTENTS

FOREWORD

*If this were a formal debate, I would be declared
the winner and we would all go home.*

The speaker was the Pacific Research Institute's Steven
Hayward, in a public forum on school choice at the
University of California at Davis Law School on April 30,
1992. No one rose to challenge Mr. Hayward. That was
because the previous speaker, representing California
school boards, announced, contrary to what many suppose, that his organization thought choice was indeed a
good thing and was actually in favor of it within certain
limits. For Mr. Hayward, that meant the debate was over,
at least in its intellectual dimension.

But it was the statement of the school board representative that proved the real shocker. Acknowledgment
that choice is a good thing is a relatively recent development for any sector of the educational establishment.
Consider, for example, the following statement from the
Association of California School Administrators, which
came in response to a choice program in the 1970s:

> *"Parental choice" proceeds from the belief that
> the purpose of education is to provide individual
> students with an education. In fact, educating
> the individual is but a means to the true end of
> education, which is to create a viable social order
> to which individuals contribute and by which
> they are sustained. "Family choice," is, therefore,
> basically selfish and anti-social in that it focuses
> on the "wants" of a single family rather than the
> "needs" of a society.*

It may come as a revelation to many parents that in the minds of administrators the purpose of school is not, after all, to provide their children with an education. This blatantly totalitarian statement only tells many parents what they already know—that the current public system has failed, both to educate their children and even in many cases to "socialize" them.

Consider the following views on public education from *Mandate for Change,* published in late 1992 by the Progressive Policy Institute. (The PPI is the think tank of the Democratic Leadership Council, and President Clinton warmly endorses its work.)

American public schools, this volume says, are "failing to meet new standards of performance being set by our global competitors." SAT scores remain below the level of the early 1960s, and in spite of funding increases of 36 percent (adjusted for inflation) there has generally been "little or no improvement" over the past decade.

Moreover, "our public school districts display in classic form the overcentralization and bureaucratic rigidity that afflicts government in general. Their inability to adapt to new circumstances and to the public demand for improvement is rooted in the monopoly character of the system."

The system takes its customers for granted and operates "without consequences for failure," and "everyone is protected except the children." Unless something quite unusual happens, "the students and the revenues will be there anyway." Thus, there is no incentive to improve. For a country that claims to be serious about education, the writers conclude, "this is an absurd arrangement."

Such judgments sound like the conservative attacks on public education that have been common since *A Nation at Risk.* That landmark 1983 study concluded that if American education did not improve, the United States would plummet to second-rate status. A strong case can be made that in key areas of business and industry this has already happened. It takes what Martin Peretz of the *New Republic* calls "cognitive dissonance" to deny the failure, apparent on every hand. This failure has led some even in the educational establishment to give a nod to choice, at least in principle. In America, nobody wants to be perceived to be against choice.

President Clinton and his wife Hillary, for example, though staunch supporters of the public system and opponents of educational vouchers, confirmed the value of choice by their decision to send their daughter Chelsea to Sidwell Friends School, a prestigious private academy operated by a religious group in Washington D.C. Like the Clintons, many parents have the means to choose the education their children receive. The working poor and people in the inner cities do not enjoy such choice, but many would like to, and the debate increasingly centers on them. What choices will they have, if any?

In May of 1992, Pacific Research Institute gathered together a number of people who have thought long and hard about these issues, on all sides. Most of the material in this book is based on that conference. It is my hope that these "voices on choice" will give you a fair and balanced understanding of the issues.

Sally Pipes, president
Pacific Research Institute for Public Policy

October 1993

PREFACE

In the current debate over education, partisan voices on school choice ring out on every hand. It is difficult, however, to find statements both for and against school choice in the same place. This volume provides the reader with a lively sampling of both from a wide variety of professional perspectives, some drawn from a conference on school choice that the Pacific Research Institute for Public Policy held in May of 1992. Included are academics, bureaucrats, politicians, union leaders, economists, lawyers, and activists—some of them parents with young children in school.

To take the debate out of the abstract, we begin with Wisconsin State Representative Polly Williams, an African American single parent who twice headed the campaigns of Jesse Jackson. Williams noted that the Reverend Jackson, like a number of public school teachers, sent his children to private schools. She wanted inner city parents to have the same option. In spite of much official opposition, Williams' Milwaukee choice program survived and is now in its third year. Clint Bolick of the Institute for Justice, who successfully defended Williams' choice program in court, describes the battle against Wisconsin's educational establishment.

Maxine Waters, a Democratic congresswoman for Los Angeles, gives her very different view on the results of choice. Waters believes that choice will allow schools to discriminate against the poor, the disabled, the difficult to educate, and ultimately will disenfranchise the urban poor. Warren Furutani, a member and past president of the Los Angeles City Board of Education, expresses a similar view.

Allubmi Indian Ben Chavis, former professor of

American Indian Studies at San Francisco State University, says he is "offended when people tell me that school choice will discriminate against me." Chavis sees school choice as eliminating the "discrimination excuse."

Professor Terry Moe of Stanford University and the Hoover Institution is concerned that the United States has not brought the experience of Great Britain into the American debate. Professor Moe examined the 1988 Education Reform Act and found that once they got used to school choice, British parents both expected it and demanded it.

Voucher proponent and former Secretary of Education William Bennett points out that federal Pell grants may be used at private and even religious schools. "All parents, regardless of income," Bennett says, "should be able to choose places where they know their children will learn." Public money, Bennett says, "should be for the education of the public, and a child in a Catholic, Methodist, or Jewish school is every bit as much a member of the public as a child in a state-supported school."

California State Assemblywoman Delaine Eastin was the author of a bill for "charter schools," which allows limited choice within the government monopoly system. Here Eastin questions the practice of improving schools by using business practices such as competition. John Mockler, who advises public schools and teachers, issues similar warnings.

Joseph Alibrandi, CEO of Whittaker Corporation and chairman of the Excellence Through Choice in Education League (ExCEL), sees intellectual capital becoming evermore important in today's competitive world. Alibrandi makes the case that the public schools are failing students by not providing that capital.

Likewise, Nobel laureate Milton Friedman, currently a senior research fellow at the Hoover Institution, wonders why the United States is first class in higher education but third class in elementary and secondary schooling. For Friedman the answer is the lack of competition at the lower levels, for which his solution is a voucher plan.

Any such plan must confront those who (other than parents and students themselves) have the biggest stake in school choice—unionized teachers. For Ralph Flynn, head of the 250,000 member California Teachers Association, the issue is a simple one. He represents California's union teachers who "do not believe that choice is in their interests." The union, thus, in its own words "vehemently" opposes California's Proposition 174, the school choice initiative. We also include materials on school choice from the CTA and its parent company, the 2.1 million member National Education Association, which has surpassed the Teamsters as the largest and most powerful union in the United States.

Though those represented here hold sharply different opinions on various ballot measures currently before voters, particularly California's Proposition 174, they do have something in common. All our contributors proclaim the same goal—to improve the quality of education and ensure a better future for our children. They are also united in that none of them was willing to defend the performance of the current government monopoly system of education. With the exception of the union representatives, all appear to agree with Wilbert Smith, an African American member of the Pasadena Unified School District Board of Education, who notes that "if we continue to do what we have always done, we are going to continue to get what we already have."

Kenneth Lloyd Billingsley

SCHOOL CHOICE PROMOTES EDUCATIONAL EXCELLENCE IN THE AFRICAN AMERICAN COMMUNITY

Parental involvement or school choice or vouchers—whatever you want to call it—is a subject very near and dear to my heart. What we did in Milwaukee was empower our parents so they could make decisions that they felt were best for their children. I enjoy having a chance to share what we have done and to say to everyone that they can do the same thing. If we can do it in Milwaukee, it can happen anywhere on the face of this earth. The choice program has really put Milwaukee on the map.

We are in the second year of the program, and we have approximately 550 students in the program now.

Polly Williams

Polly Williams, a Wisconsin State Representative, sponsored the Milwaukee school choice legislation.

This is adapted from a speech at the Heritage Foundation presented during their Black History Month series in 1992.

1

The first year we had approximately 420 students whose parents opted to get into the program. But because immediately after the bill was passed we were sued by the teachers' union, a lot of parents dropped out. They were afraid because they were poor that the powerful union would beat them. The parents said they were going to put their kids back in the public schools because they were afraid that when they lost in the courts they were going to be stuck with no school for their kids. But we won.

When the bill passed, we did not know that what we had done was historic. Most of the time, when poor people accomplish things nobody even mentions it. We have been struggling and fighting all of our lives; we never get any real national front-page coverage. Our own state's largest newspaper did not even run the story. Since our own newspapers did not even recognize our victory, we just went on with our business.

And then I got a call from Clint Bolick at the Landmark Legal Foundation. He wanted to let me know that if I needed any help, he was there to assist me. Now, we did not know at the time that we were going to need any help, because we did not know that we had done anything to upset people. I just thanked him for calling, but I did not think I would need to call him back. And it turns out we had to call him right away, because the teachers' union immediately took us to court. It shook up the teachers' union that we had help from someone in Washington, D.C.

We have made several court appearances over the issue of funding. The teachers' unions say that we are not supposed to take public dollars for private schools, that to do so is unconstitutional and illegal. The fact that the program is helping low-income students and that those students are succeeding has never been the issue for the teachers' union. They maintain that we are not supposed to take public money. How will they hold their captive audience and keep teachers employed if parents begin to take their kids out of school and get them educated? The one thing you cannot have is kids coming out of your schools educated, because then what are the teachers going to do?

We know that if the Supreme Court rules against us the children who are currently being educated—children who are learning, children who are being successfully educated—are going to be put back into a bankrupt system where they surely will fail. It is going to take a lot for the court to do that, given the fact that they have to look into the faces of these parents and say,

If we can accept the fact that Communism can fall after seventy- some years, I do not see why we cannot stand and fight a bureaucracy that is doing a terrible job, that is harming our children, and that is hurting this whole country.

"We're taking your child and putting him back in that bankrupt system where we know he is going to fail, and we are taking him out of this place because he is being educated." It is a hard decision for the State Supreme Court to make.* To me, the issue is very simple. It is a good program, the kids are learning, leave them alone.

The parents are saying that they are not going to tolerate their children being miseducated anymore, and that they are the ones who are ultimately responsible for what happens to their children. The parents are going to be the ones who will stick together and stand up and fight.

---

*In March of 1992 the Wisconsin Supreme Court ruled the Milwaukee School Choice program permissible under the state's constitution.

They are going to do it because they have people like me, Landmark Legal Foundation, and others who are there to say, "We are with you to help you help your own children." And it is only when we come together and fight the bureaucracy that we can get what we need, because if the bureaucracy refuses to be responsible to us, then we are not obligated to maintain support. If we can accept what happened in Eastern Europe, if we can accept the fact that Communism can fall after seventy-some years, I do not see why we cannot stand and fight a bureaucracy that is doing a terrible job, that is harming our children, and that is hurting this whole country.

When we have children who walk across the stage at graduation and cannot read and write, that hurts all of us.

In my school district we have a 90 percent failure rate. Now, how do you tolerate a 90 percent failure rate every year, with $6,000 a year of taxpayers' dollars being misspent to fund failure? Some 14.9 percent of the Milwaukee freshmen who enter our high schools do not graduate from 12th grade. And of those who remain in school and walk across the stage and pick up that certificate of attendance, only 10 percent of those children can read that piece of paper—10 percent. And we are tolerating this situation in our public schools.

And the reason for it is not the system or the school, it is the parents. It is people like me. It is single, poor, socially deprived people. If your children come out of a home like my home—my husband and I divorced very early—the kids are supposedly doomed. My son is the one male in a household of four or five women; if you listen to the social critics, he's supposed to be in jail right now. My son is 35 years old and all of my children have successfully finished school, are doing well, have never been in trouble with the law, and you are calling me to speak to you. Yet I am one of those people who is supposed to be very stupid because I am black, I live in the inner city, I am poor, and

I raised my children in a single parent home. Well, those are lies.

The only thing different about us is that we have been deprived of resources and access. When you empower parents like me, there is a major difference. We become responsible for our own lives. We want to be responsible for ourselves. We are sick and tired of dependency on social programs that take away all of our will, motivation, and drive.

We want what everybody else wants. We want to be self-sufficient. We want to have equal access to all of the resources in society and then begin to decide for ourselves what we want. It is like James Brown said, "We don't want anybody givin' us anything." We just want you to open up the door and we'll get it ourselves. It is then up to us to learn how to gain access to the system.

We are going to make mistakes. Another thing our saviors want to do is save us from ourselves. We cannot make any mistakes. Well, if you do not make mistakes, there is no learning. We have been living too much with everyone else's mistakes. We need to learn from our own mistakes.

> *When you empower parents like me, there is a major difference. We become responsible for our own lives. We want to be responsible for ourselves. We are sick and tired of dependency on social programs that take away all of our will, motivation, and drive... We want to be empowered, and that is what the choice program has done... And parents are running to get into this program.*

5

We want to be empowered, and that is what the choice program has done. It has empowered low-income families to take control and decide for themselves what they want for their children. And we have taken control of that state dollar that was going into the public school system that was failing the child. Now, the parents of over a thousand low-income children have a choice. If you are poor, you can get into this program; 1,000 kids can go to a private, nonsectarian school located in Milwaukee. And parents are running to get into this program.

Poor people want the same things for their children that people with money want. We all want our children to be successful, because when our children achieve we feel good. And when our children fail, we feel bad. We know that for low-income families the only way out of poverty is education. We want our children educated. I do not know any poor parents who do not want their children educated. Some of us do not know how to go about accessing the system. We need to begin to help parents and give them information; then they can make a determination about what they want to do.

Because of the lack of information, a lot of our children are failing in school, because their parents do not know what their rights are. And that is what we are doing—informing the parents so they know what their rights are, and making sure that those resources are made available to them. If the funds are allocated equally, then those people who are having a problem will find a solution. We did. We went to the parents and said, "Look, we have this problem. We are going to try to make an alternative for you, but you have to come and you have to work. You have to make that commitment to help your own children." And parents came. That is the thing that shocked the bureaucracy, because they could never get parents to come to a meeting. But we had meetings with 200 to 300 parents attending.

And what a beautiful rose garden of color. I did not know Milwaukee had that many whites, Hispanics, Asians, and Indian people until we started calling our meetings. They came to our meetings because these people cared. And the schools are racially integrated. We did not have any law that you have to have racial balance. We didn't even include that in the bill. In fact, my friends were saying that we had to make sure that the schools were racially balanced. I said, "No, these schools are not under court order and we are not letting you put them under court order, because these schools focus on education not desegregation transportation."

We are going to educate these kids. We don't care what color they are. We are not counting to see how many blacks, how many whites, how many Asians, and how many Indians. Race has got nothing to do with what we do. The public schools are too busy counting to see how many blacks and how many whites are enrolled.

Everything is based on how to get more money from the bureaucracy, not on how to educate the children. This situation is sustaining the tension between the races. Milwaukee has also been designated as one of the most racist cities in the country. It is things like racial quotas in the schools that are creating the problem, because they make decisions exclusively on the race of the child. How do you think a parent feels when they tell him that his child is the wrong color and that is why that child cannot get into a good school? We have a 30 percent white population, so that leftover 70 percent is constantly running, fighting, chasing, and worrying about how to get into a good school. That does not make sense.

The "educrats" and "socialcrats" who are making those decisions do not have their children in public schools. Their children are enrolled safely in private or parochial schools. These officials are experimenting with all of our lives, but only as long as their kids are safely away. They

> *The bureaucracy is supposed to do what parents want, not parents doing what the bureaucracy wants.*

are messing with our kids. We have to stop all those kinds of decisions that erode and harm our community.

I am not a system's person. I am not a bureaucrat; I work outside the bureaucracy. Even my own party has a problem with me. You need someone who is not a part of the bureaucracy to break the mold. I have already demonstrated that I will break the mold, that I will make decisions based on the needs of the people, that I listen to the people. I do not care about the system or the bureaucracy; if it is not working, I will break it down.

I have learned that you have got to seize the time, you have to be able to act, and if you listen to what people are saying, you will act right. Everything we have done in this fight and struggle to get the choice bill passed worked because we listened to the people. It was important that we hear the parents, and I heard them. I know; I live with the parents. I understand their pain. I know as a parent myself how it feels to be helpless and not in control of what happens to your children and yourself.

Any time we can empower parents, empower people, that is more important than anything. And when we start talking about the government, we forget that we are the ones who vote for those who pass the laws. Look, if it is a bad law and it is impacting negatively on us, the elected officials had better change it or we are going to change them. We have to make things work for ourselves, because in the end it comes down to you and your family and what is happening to you at home. You cannot sit around and wait for somebody else to come and make things better for you. You have to get into that race right away and stand up and fight.

Our children, particularly low-income, ethnic minority children, need to see their parents in responsible, powerful positions, so they can feel better about themselves. Every chance I get I make sure the kids in my neighborhood see me standing tall and arguing and fighting to let them know I am standing up for them. When I come home they say, "Miss Polly, I saw you on television." It is very seldom that kids from my neighborhood can look at television or read a newspaper and see people they know; so they feel good about seeing their neighbor. Or when I come home and I have loads of groceries, the kids all converge on me, "Miss Polly, let me take your groceries in." They are really proud and happy to be able to do something to help people.

Parents have the right to decide on the quality and the type of education their children receive. If their kids need a private, parochial, and independent school education, they have the right to make that decision, and their taxpayer dollars ought to go where they want their children educated, and not to some bureaucracy that says they know better.

We have got to have these models for our kids, but more important, we have to have parents in charge of their children. The only way the problems in the schools are going to change is if parents take charge and take their rightful positions as the authority over their children. The bureaucracy is supposed to do

9

what parents want, not parents doing what the bureaucracy wants.

We have to stop handing our children over to bureaucrats who decide to pass laws based on their needs and families. The parental choice bill that we passed is a bill that helped parents get involved with their kids, because parents made a commitment to help their children. The public schools were not helping parents and these private, nonsectarian schools are.

If any of you saw "60 Minutes," you saw little Larry. Larry did return. He returned to Urban Day School in September 1991 where he was a 1.0 student. He did not want to leave with a 1.5 average. He is now a 4.0 student. He wanted to leave that school at the top of the class. Little Larry has had four offers of scholarships to pay for his college education. Well, little Larry is set, there is money now to help him.

We have a lot of students like little Larry in these inner-city schools, and we need opportunity and choice for these students. We need to aim everything we do, and make all resources available, to save our children. Because if we don't put the emphasis and focus on our children, none of us is safe. Parents have the right to decide on the quality and the type of education their children receive. If their kids need a private, parochial, and independent school education, they have the right to make that decision, and their taxpayer dollars ought to go where they want their children educated, and not to some bureaucracy that says they know better.

CHOICE WILL DEVASTATE OUR URBAN SCHOOLS

NO

The American public school system is responsible for the education of approximately 90 percent of our nation's children. Therefore, the last thing this country can afford to do is divert scarce resources from our already hurting public schools to fund private school education. That is what would happen under school "voucher" plans, supported by many leading Republicans and other conservatives.

As states experience budgetary crises, we must decide and act on meaningful reforms that will enable our educational system to better respond to the needs of our young people. "Choice" is not a reform—it is an

Maxine Waters

Maxine Waters is a Democratic congresswoman from Los Angeles.

From *False Choices*, published by Rethinking Schools, 1001 E. Keefe Ave., Milwaukee, WI 53212. (414) 964-9646. Reprinted with permission.

> *Private schools are not governed by federal, state, or community public policies. While some might wield this fact to support expanding choice to include private schools, such a move will simply amount to an open season on the hard-won civil rights gains our country has made in the last 30 years.*

abandonment of American children and teachers who rely on our public system for education and job opportunities. Contrary to claims, school choice will be devastating for urban, minority, and poor students who desperately need quality education.

Private schools are not governed by federal, state, or community public policies. While some might wield this fact to support expanding choice to include private schools, such a move will simply amount to an open season on the hard-won civil rights gains our country has made in the last 30 years. Private schools, for instance, are free to discriminate—they may accept anyone by their own choosing. And you can be sure that those who will be rejected will be students who require higher cost services such as special or remedial education.

The recently passed and widely acclaimed Americans with Disabilities Act, civil rights legislation, and laws governing the use of defamatory materials have no bearing on the functioning of private schools; and if students should misbehave, fail to perform adequately, or simply not fit the mold, no uniform standard shall regulate how their cases will be handled—opening the floodgates for preferential treatment.

Our taxpayers' dollars should not be used to support privately owned, elite academies. Neither should taxpayers support sectarian institutions or religious schools, as prohibited by our constitutional mandate separating church and state.

Tragically, at a time when our children need and deserve serious, thoughtful, and dramatic change, the best that "choice" advocates can do is offer a smoke screen that diverts attention and resources from our nation's poorest "at-risk" students.

A NATIVE AMERICAN PERSPECTIVE ON CHOICE

I would like to share my perspective of school choice and, in particular, look at school choice from an American Indian perspective. I am an American Indian. I am Allumbi from North Carolina. I come from a very traditional family, and if you understand anything about American Indians, you know that we are traditional and that being traditional means being conservative.

I come from a very large family. I have twelve brothers and sisters. As you can imagine, my dad's a pretty good businessman. In school, I was an average student but not a very good student. I attended an all Indian school system from

Ben Chavis

Ben Chavis is an Allumbi Indian and former assistant professor of American Indian Studies at San Francisco State University.

Adapted from the conference proceedings of "Rebuilding California's Schools, The Educational Choice Debate," May 1, 1992, San Francisco, CA, sponsored by the Pacific Research Institute.

15

As you well know, we American Indians are not in control of that many institutions. School choice would allow us—and at that time it did allow us—to control an institution called education, which is a very powerful institution.

1st through 5th grade, and then in 6th through 12th grade I attended an integrated school system. Looking back on it, I think this sparked my interest in choice when I got older.

I saw a big difference in the two school systems. Being raised in North Carolina I was forced to attend an integrated school system. I had no choice. Although I was an average and not good student, I was allowed to go to college because I was an excellent athlete. But upon arriving at college I discovered I had not been prepared to enter college. I had a choice of which college I wanted to attend. I had a choice of which area I wanted to study, and that changed my whole life. I chose to pursue education because I realized what an inadequate education I had received in the integrated school system.

My tribe is unique. In 1885 we started our own school system in North Carolina. It was community-based. All of our teachers were Indian. All our principals were Indian. Our school board members were Indian. This allowed us an opportunity to develop our own system, to be in control of our own destiny, which is rare among American Indians. This continued until 1970.

In 1966, a graduate student from Duke University doing his dissertation on my tribe noted that we had the highest number of educated Indians in America. If you took all the Indians who, for example, entered education,

16

we had more than all the other tribes put together, yet we were only the fifth largest tribe in the U.S. I think part of our success was because we had our own school system.

We had the highest number of high school graduates. We had the lowest percentage of high school dropouts. Our students scored at the highest level of any American Indian students in the nation. We were in control of our system—I attribute our excellent results to that fact. North Carolina required school integration in 1970. They dismantled our school system. The dropout rate increased.

> I am offended when people tell me that school choice will discriminate against me. What does the public school system do now?

I did my Ph.D. dissertation on this in the 1980s. I compared two school systems, an integrated system and an Indian school system. I discovered that for those students who attended an Indian school system—an all Indian school system designed for American Indians, controlled by American Indians, with Indian principals, with an Indian superintendent, with an all Indian school board—the dropout rate increased significantly when we transferred over to integration. Also, the unemployment rate started to soar.

Economically we started to suffer. As you well know, we American Indians are not in control of that many institutions. School choice would allow us—and at that time it did allow us—to control an institution called education, which is a very powerful institution. I am offended when people tell me that school choice will discriminate against me. What does the public school system do now? In North Carolina, after integration what was the result?

> *School choice would empower my community. Minorities can be empowered by choice because they can start their own school system. We have the skills.*

We lost control of our school system and the number of Allumbi Indians who went off to college started to decrease.

We also had our own university. It's called Pembrook State University. It's a teachers college; the only one in the nation. My tribe was in control of it. I have a Ph.D. in education. I've been a principal, elementary teacher, junior high teacher, high school teacher, counselor, and a grant writer. Yet I cannot get a job in my community because we no longer control the university. We no longer control the school system.

How would school choice work? First of all, I could start my own school system designed for my own people. I could return home. I wouldn't be lost in San Francisco. I'm 3,000 miles away from home, and my parents wonder, "When are you going to come home?"

School choice would empower my community. Minorities can be empowered by choice because they can start their own school systems. We have the skills, and if we are in control of our own school system we cannot use the excuse that we have been discriminated against.

When I attended an all Indian school system, I sat next to my relatives. We worked together. The teachers understood my background. They also knew my parents. When I played hooky (which I occasionally did), on Sunday it was "Where was Ben? He didn't go to school on Thursday."

I love Mark Twain's work. In *Life on the Mississippi* Twain talks about growing up on the river and having to learn all the sandbars and know where all the snags were—how he had to know that river. This experience reminds me of the public school system; they try to teach us the basics too. But Mark Twain pointed out another thing—-he said, the river is always changing. And education must change too. The education provided for my people is inadequate. American Indians score at the bottom of any test used to evaluate ability. At the bottom! Why would I support any system that places us at the bottom?

> *The education provided for my people is inadequate. American Indians score at the bottom of any test used to evaluate ability. At the bottom! Why would I support any system that places us at the bottom?*

Those who have a grasp of American history may recall how the United States denied American Indian people citizenship until the late 1920s. We were the last to be considered citizens of the U.S. The state of Arizona would not allow American Indians the right to vote and to participate in the democratic process until the late 1940s. In North Carolina, American Indians were denied the choice to intermarry with non-Indians until the late 1960s. In each case, the decisions were justified by suggesting that American Indians would be taken advantage of by others if allowed citizenship, if allowed the right to vote, or if allowed to intermarry. This was such a common practice used to control and oppress American Indians that it was referred to as paternalism. In fact, some in academia have made a career out of investigating this phenomenon created by the government toward American Indians.

It is interesting to note in 1992 that public schools

and the national, state, and local education associations are using a similar argument against school choice.

Are American Indians expecting too much by requesting a quality education or considering school choice as an alternative to the public education system that is not addressing the needs of our American Indian children?

That's the question.

A BATTLE FOR THE SOUL OF PUBLIC EDUCATION

When we talk about choice in California, we are talking about a mortal battle for the fundamental soul of public education in a democratic society. That is what the fight is about.

It is no coincidence that funding for public education is receding as our school districts become more populated by children of color. It is no coincidence that dollars are being pulled from our underfunded, overburdened school system at the same time our governor and the president of this nation are pushing vouchers and choice as an education alternative for the middle class. What took place in California will take place in your state as well.

Warren Furutani

Warren Furutani is a member and past president of the Los Angeles City Board of Education.

From *False Choices,* published by Rethinking Schools, 1001 E. Keefe Ave., Milwaukee, WI 53212. (414) 964-9646. Reprinted with permission.

It is clear that vouchers and choice will be a vehicle for those who have the mobility and the additional dollars to go to the private sector... Those who are left behind, those with special needs, special challenges, different languages, those whom we've been failing for generations, will be relegated to the backseat of society for the rest of their lives. We cannot accept that.

It is clear that vouchers and choice will be a vehicle for those who have the mobility and the additional dollars to go to the private sector— while at the same time guaranteeing that those who can't augment that voucher will then be relegated to an underfunded, overburdened system. And it will be a system that has been deserted by the middle class, deserted by those who think they are getting better for their own but who in fact are eliminating one of the most fundamental democratic institutions in our country— public education.

As administrators and school boards in urban districts are, like their students, increasingly people of color, and as people of color become more of a force in our urban centers, we find that those who sit in seats of state and federal power are trying to pull away the middle class. They are deserting public education. As a result, those who are left behind, those with special needs, special challenges, different languages, those whom we've been failing for generations, will be relegated to the backseat of society for the rest of their lives. We cannot accept that.

THE BRITISH BATTLE FOR CHOICE

YES

Several years ago the British enacted the Educational Reform Act, legislation that is a coherent and very radical version of the kinds of things American reformers are talking about. Now, after several years, they have real experience with how these things work themselves out in practice. I think it's important for people concerned about reforming education in the United States to learn what we can about how these reforms work. Here we have a whole nation engaged in radical reform, and it ought to be an integral part of our debate. So far it hasn't been.

In 1991, the *Sunday Times* of London invited

Terry Moe

Terry Moe is a senior fellow at the Hoover Institution and professor of political science at Stanford University. He co-author (with John Chubb) Politics, Markets & America's Schools, *published by the Brookings Institution.*

Adapted from the conference proceedings of "Rebuilding California's Schools, The Educational Choice Debate," May 1, 1992, San Francisco, CA, sponsored by the Pacific Research Institute.

John Chubb and I out to look at their schools and arrive at a preliminary assessment of what's going on and how well the act seems to be working. We were eager to do that. We talked to academics, policymakers, school heads, and many other people directly involved in British schooling.

British schools are experiencing the same problems we have here. People complain about poor performance and poor quality in the schools—their dropout rate is absolutely horrendous. Two-thirds of their kids drop out of school by the age of sixteen. Very few kids graduate, and the inequities are glaring. It's clear that middle class and upper middle class kids have far better educational opportunities than lower class kids do. And the people there want to do something about it.

In the early days they focused on the obvious things: on more money, on raising the requirements, on getting better teachers, and so on. And after a while they began to say, as we did here, that those things don't work. They realized that the system needed to be fundamentally changed. So they began to talk about restructuring, and they focused on three basic kinds of reforms: school-based management, choice, and accountability—the same sorts of reforms Americans talk about. It's really quite remarkable how similar the movements have been in the two countries. The difference is, they actually followed through.

The Education Reform Act of 1988 built legislative reform around school-based management, choice, and accountability. I want to focus on choice, because choice is far and away the most radical component of this package. If the Education Reform Act is going to prove successful in reforming their system, it will be because of the role of choice, not because of school-based management or accountability.

The three elements of their choice program are open enrollment, City Technology Colleges, and an "opting out" procedure in which the schools can leave the Local Education Authority (LEA) and go out on their own—although they remain public. Opting-out in particular is wonderfully subversive. It threatens to completely transform the system, and everybody knows it. As a result, this is the reform that is absolutely unacceptable to the establishment. They have gone all out to stop choice, and in particular, opting out.

The irony here is that the one reform that really promises to transform the system in a way that can bring about significant change and significant improvement is precisely the reform that generates intense opposition—to the point where, over the long haul, it may well be stopped. The reforms that are far more likely to be put in place are those that aren't going to work very well. This is exactly the situation in the United States as well. Here, school-based management and accountability are the sorts of things that all reformers can get happy about and get involved in. Choice is another matter. The powerful members of the educational establishment—unions, superintendents, school board members, and education schools—are all 100 percent opposed to it.

Real choice changes the system, transforming it into

Opting-out in particular is wonderfully subversive. It threatens to completely transform the system, and everybody knows it. As a result, this is the reform that is absolutely unacceptable to the establishment. They have gone all out to stop choice, and in particular, opting out.

Choice is another matter. The educational establishment—union, superintendents, school board members, and education schools—are all 100 percent opposed to it. Real choice changes the system, transforming it into something else. They don't want that. Choice is different, and that structures the politics of education.

something else. They don't want that. Choice is different, and that structures the politics of education.

Let me turn now to open enrollment, which they've actually had in Britain for the last ten years or so. The Education Reform Act made it more difficult for the LEAs to manipulate open enrollment to their own advantage. In the beginning, the LEAs were saying, yes, you can have choice, but all the good schools are full and a lot of you people have to go to the bad schools. We don't want them to be under-enrolled. So they were actually stage-managing things—using the fact that there is a fixed supply of schools, and they were the ones, of course, who fixed the supply. The Education Reform Act reduced their discretion and thereby expanded the true scope of parental choice.

What has the experience been under the act? First, while parents were initially confused by their new responsibilities, they quickly adapted to them—and came to demand choice as a right. Donald Naismith, Chief Education Officer for the borough of Wandsworth in London, puts it this way: "The argument is won. People like and want choice. Having experienced it now for some years, they are addicted to it. There is no going back."

Second, research shows that people are not frivolous in the way they exercise choice, and they are not uninformed. They take action to get informed because the information really means something to them and to their kids. Also, the criteria that they use are not frivolous. They are not choosing schools on the basis of sports or uniforms. They are choosing schools primarily on the basis of three criteria: discipline and order, achievement, and proximity. In other words, they want the best school close to home—which is exactly what you'd expect.

> *"The argument is won. People like and want choice. Having experienced it now for some years, they are addicted to it. There is no going back."*
> —Donald Naismith, Chief Education Officer for the borough of Wandsworth in London

Finally, the incentives seem to be working right. The heads of schools that are oversubscribed are really proud of it. They talk at length about all the great things they are doing to promote their schools and attract students. The heads of schools that are undersubscribed are apologetic and embarrassed. They talk about all the reforms they're going to adopt to attract more kids to their schools. There's a real competitive feeling in the schools now that was never there before. It's due to choice.

Nonetheless, there is a basic problem here: The British have created an open enrollment system in which there is very little to choose from, because the supply of schools is controlled by the LEAs. That is the Achilles' heel of this act.

Opting out is of vital importance—but it does not change the supply of schools. What opting out does is allow for existing schools to leave the LEAs. The number of schools remains the same; it is just that these new schools are more autonomous. In fact, they are almost completely autonomous, so they are far better able to create the kinds of organizations they want to create, and that's crucial. As of now (May 1992), about 150 schools have opted out, which is a tiny fraction of the total.

In the beginning, schools lived in fear of the kind of reaction they would get, primarily from the Labour party and the establishment, if they tried to opt out. Now that the Conservatives have won the election, however, things are somewhat improved. Everybody we talked to said that if the Conservatives win many schools will likely consider opting out.

Initially, a lot of schools opted out because they were threatened with closure or change of character by the LEAs. They were trying to escape. But over time it became clear that all kinds of schools were beginning to opt out for two main reasons: money and autonomy. When a school opts out, they get the same per child allotment that any school gets. But the other schools get their money funneled through the LEAs, which keep about 16 percent of the money for administrative expenses.

The schools that opt out get that 16 percent—which the LEAs lose. In return, the schools don't get to use the LEA services, but what the schools say is that they don't want many of those services anyway. They want the 16 percent to buy books and computers and other things for their schools. If they want to buy certain services, they can buy them from their LEA or from another LEA or from a private contractor. So that is a major motivation to opt out. Note that there is no extra money involved here. They are getting money that was always there. It was just spent by somebody else. Now they get to spend it.

One of the main reasons schools don't opt out is politics. There are strong inducements for many schools to opt out. We talked to a number of heads within the system who told us: "Look, we would love to opt out. The LEAs are nothing but trouble, and we don't value their services. We can't even fix the windows and paint the building without their approval. They won't give it to us. They won't give us any money. It's horrible. We want out, but we can't get out because we're afraid of what will happen." And what will happen is politics.

One of the first schools to opt out was Small Heath, in a very poor area of Birmingham. Their clientele consists mainly of immigrants, many of them from Pakistan and Bangladesh. These people are often unemployed, but they have very strong families and place a great deal of emphasis on education. They felt that their LEA was entirely insensitive to their special needs, and they wanted to opt out. They went to their Labour-controlled LEA, the people who normally claim to represent poor people and minorities, and said: "We'd like to control our own school." Labour and the establishment said, "No way; this is our system, and you are going to stay within it."

But they went ahead and started the opting out procedure. They voted to opt out. Then all hell broke loose. Labour and the establishment went on the warpath against them. They went door-to-door lobbying parents and distributing leaflets. They launched a media campaign against the head of the school, slandering his character and claiming that he was anti-Muslim. Actually, he is an expert on the Muslim culture and revered by these people. It was a very nasty campaign. Ultimately, they went ahead and opted out anyway. But the lesson was clear—any school that's going to opt out is going to be threatened with severe costs by Labour and the establishment, because maintaining the system is more important to them than helping the poor. This intense

> *But the lesson was clear—any school that's going to opt out is going to be threatened with severe costs by Labour and the establishment, because maintaining the system is more important to them than helping the poor. This intense opposition from their alleged "friends" keeps a lot of schools within the system.*

opposition from their alleged "friends" keeps a lot of schools within the system.

When schools do opt out, what happens? The standard criticism is that it is unmanageable. They can't handle it. It's inequitable. The fact is, it doesn't look that way at all. The heads of these schools say they're doing great. In fact, they say "it's a piece of cake" and "it's the most natural thing in the world." Autonomy seems to be very good for schools. They've done tremendous amounts for their own facilities, buying all sorts of new equipment and materials. These places have been transformed, and they are finally able to hire the kinds of people that they want. As one head put it, "I only hire teachers who burn to teach." He has complete control over that, and he hires teachers who share the mission of the school. They create a team. In other schools, where the teachers are forced on the school head, there is no team—just a bunch of people who happen to work in the same place.

What about equity? The standard charge is that the opted out schools are skimming the cream. But it isn't like that at all. For instance, Baverstock is in a poor area of

Birmingham. They have done so well as an opted out school that everybody wants to go there. Middle class kids want to transfer in, but Baverstock is forced to screen them out in favor of the local kids. Baverstock would rather have the local kids because what they want is a community school in which parents are supportive. Parents come to painting parties and gardening parties. They are there all the time. The buildings are open at night. Parents and local community people watch the school to protect against vandalism. The whole point of this school, its mission, is to build a quality institution for the local community—and most certainly not to skim the cream.

They are choosing schools primarily on the basis of three criteria: discipline and order, achievement, and proximity. In other words, they want the best school close to home—which is exactly what you'd expect.

What does the future hold for the British reforms? The basic problem is that they have no mechanism for increasing the supply of schools, and this needs to be remedied. One way to do this is to allow private schools to "opt in," and there is a bill in the House of Lords proposing just that. Another method is to adopt something like the charter schools program that we have here in California, where teachers are allowed to form their own autonomous schools.

In these and other ways, can the British complete their revolution and construct a coherent choice system, instead of a compartmentalized set of reforms?

The answer is unclear. On the one hand, the Labour

> When the American poor rise up and say, "We demand a new kind of educational system that gives us the right to leave bad schools and seek out good ones" the Democrats and the establishment groups claiming to represent them will close ranks in fierce opposition. So the poor have to look elsewhere. Where do they look?
> In Milwaukee they looked to the Republican governor, Tommy Thompson, and to businesses and to conservatives.

party can be no help at all. It supports the massive educational bureaucracy, it is tightly allied with the educational establishment, and it has no intention of endorsing radical change. Although it claims to speak for poor people, when these same people rise up and say, "We want out," it will oppose them.

Ironically, only the Conservative party can be expected to support the poor in transforming British education. So now you have an odd situation. The traditional progressives have become the conservatives, and the conservatives have become the progressives—the only source of potential change in the institutional system.

In the United States I think it's basically the same. The Democrats are stuck. They are traditionally allied very closely with the educational establishment. When proposals are made to change this system, the entire educational establishment will oppose it, and almost all Democrats will go along with them.

When the American poor rise up and say, "We demand a new kind of educational system that gives us the right to leave bad schools and seek out good ones"—as they did recently in Milwaukee—the Democrats and the establishment groups claiming to represent them will close ranks in fierce opposition. So the poor have to look elsewhere. Where do they look? In Milwaukee they looked to the Republican governor, Tommy Thompson, and to businesses and to conservatives because they are the only ones willing to transform the system.

I think the wave of the future in the politics of education is this unorthodox alliance between poor people, who desperately need change more than any other group in society, and Republicans—or in Britain the Conservatives—and business, who are the only powerful groups willing to transform the system. When these powerful groups get together, they have the capacity to overwhelm the protectors of the status quo and make the promise of choice a reality, both in Britain and in the United States.

A WORM IN THE APPLE: HOW VOUCHERS WOULD UNDERMINE LEARNING

Delaine Eastin

Delaine Eastin represents the 20th District (Fremont) in California's State Assembly and serves as chair of the Assembly's K-12 Education Committee.

Competition. It's as American as apple pie.

But would free market competition improve the quality of education for our kids? That's the question at the heart of the debate over the school voucher initiative that will appear on the state ballot this November.

If the initiative is passed, the state will provide parents with a $2,600 voucher (per child), which they can redeem at any school—public or private—where they choose to send their children.

I'm all for competition. But vouchers could turn out to be a worm in the apple of public education—that would undermine learning

Reprinted with permission of the office of Assemblywoman Delaine Eastin.

> *I'm all for competition. But vouchers could turn out to be a worm in the apple of public education—that would undermine learning and sidestep the real problems in the schools.*

and sidestep the real problems in the schools.

There are several problems with this initiative. First of all, it gives taxpayers' money to private and parochial schools, but requires practically no accountability from those schools in return. The initiative provides for no teacher accountability, no financial accountability, no educational accountability.

For example, when parents decide to switch from public to private school, can they be sure that their child's private school teacher will have a college degree—or even a high school diploma? Can they be sure that the private school is financially solvent enough to make it through the school year? Or can they even be sure that the school building is earthquake safe—and not built on a toxic waste site? In the public schools, parents are assured of some minimum standards. But there are virtually none in the private schools—and the initiative makes it nearly impossible to set standards for private schools.

The initiative won't even hold new private schools to the basic standards of equality of opportunity. In admitting students, the initiative allows private schools to discriminate on the basis of physical disability, gender, religion, or even economic status—all at taxpayers' expense. Having schools without standards won't improve learning.

Second, this initiative allows schools to fail. But it does nothing to protect taxpayers when they do. When public school systems go belly up as a result of the voucher initiative, the courts are likely to rule that taxpayers will be stuck with the tab—and it won't be cheap.

The purpose of the voucher initiative is to foster competition—so that only fit schools will survive. But when the Richmond Unified School District went bankrupt in 1989, the California courts ruled that the State was required to bail out the Richmond schools—to the tune of $29 million.

As a result of the Richmond failure, we have taken steps to make public schools more financially accountable and to prevent further bankruptcies. Despite these measures, the State Controller recently reported that 27 school districts (including the $3 billion Los Angeles Unified School District) are currently in financial trouble. Because the courts have ruled that the state must provide for the education of all children, there is reason to believe the state will be on the hook for the education of children who enroll in private schools that go bankrupt midyear.

In admitting students, the initiative allows private schools to discriminate on the basis of physical disability, gender, religion, or even economic status—all at taxpayers' expense. Having schools without standards won't improve learning.

Third, vouchers are likely to harden the racial and economic lines that divide us. The public school system has always been the most visible symbol of the American melting pot. It is in the public schools—from one-room schoolhouses to the 700-school Los Angeles Unified School District—that we as a nation have made our stand for

Finally, the voucher initiative won't deal with any of the real problems our schools face. It won't remove guns or drugs from our schools. It won't teach more kids how to read or write. It won't prepare noncollege-bound kids for jobs. It will do nothing to get parents more involved with their children's education.

equality of opportunity. But by passing this initiative, we abandon our commitment to the common good.

Other countries with far less diverse populations than our own have seen that school choice exacerbates class and racial segregation. According to a recent study in Scotland, 24 percent of children whose parents were college educated chose to leave neighborhood schools, but less than 1 percent of children whose parents had no college chose to leave.

Finally, the voucher initiative won't deal with any of the real problems our schools face. It won't remove guns or drugs from our schools. It won't teach more kids how to read or write. It won't prepare noncollege-bound kids for jobs. It will do nothing to get parents more involved with their children's education.

Our schools have real problems. They need serious reforms: higher standards, safer classrooms, more job-related training. We need parents, teachers, and school administrators to forget the turf battles that have stymied fundamental change—and get down to the real business of reform. Among the readers of these words are the children of machinists and mechanics, bricklayers and bakers, domestic workers and dress clerks who today live better than their parents did because their parents made some hard choices and supported public schools.

The voucher initiative is meant to be radical—to shake up the school system, much the same way deregulation of the savings and loan industry was meant to shake up the financial industry. But deregulating S&Ls resulted in a rotting at the core of the industry—fraud, mismanagement, and collapse, costing taxpayers $200 billion. If we allow this worm to get into our public school system, the cost won't just be in dollars but in our children's futures.

THE
WISCONSIN
CHOICE PLAN

Whenever we engage in school choice litigation we always walk the hallways and drive the neighborhoods of both the public schools and the private schools of the cities where we go. And I'll tell you, I would never, never send my little boys to the schools people in the inner cities are forced to send their kids to. People in the inner cities feel powerless in the area of education, and we have to do something about it.

What it all comes down to in the school choice area is exactly that—power, because school choice effectuates a revolution that transfers the basic power over education from bureau-

Clint Bolick

Clint Bolick is vice president and director of litigation at the Institute for Justice in Washington, D. C. He successfully defended the Milwaukee choice program before the Wisconsin Supreme Court.

Adapted from the conference proceedings of "Rebuilding California's Schools, The Educational Choice Debate," May 1, 1992, San Francisco, CA, sponsored by the Pacific Research Institute.

41

> *What it all comes down to in the school choice area is exactly that—power, because school choice effectuates a revolution that transfers the basic power over education from bureaucrats to parents.*

crats to parents. That is the one absolute that you can never take away from that concept. That is why the education establishment is fighting choice as if its livelihood depends upon it—because it does.

I had the tremendous honor to represent low-income parents in the Wisconsin court battle recently, and I experienced that reactionary frenzy on the part of the education establishment firsthand. The Milwaukee public schools are as bad as just about any schools anywhere. If you are a low-income kid in Milwaukee, you are much more likely to be murdered or a victim of violence in the schools than you are to graduate. Eighty-five percent of kids in the Milwaukee public schools from welfare families never graduate, and those who do graduate with an average GPA of "D." They fill the jails, and they fill the welfare rolls. To be low income and consigned to the Milwaukee public schools means to be consigned almost certainly to a future of poverty and despair.

That is why in 1990 Representative Polly Williams pioneered the first true choice program in the United States. It is a small program, up to 1,000 low-income kids can use their share of state education funds—$2,500 per student—at private, nonsectarian, community schools.

I visited these schools. I would be proud to send my little boys to these schools. They look different from some of the public schools in a couple of ways. You see pictures of Malcolm X on some of the walls, and they're different in another way—education goes on there. They educate low-income kids, and they give them a first rate education at less than half the cost of the public schools.

Two things happened when the parental choice program was passed and went into practice, and these same two things will happen any time you have a comprehensive choice program. The first is that immediately kids who were going to educational cesspools were allowed and empowered to go to good schools. Not a lot in the Milwaukee case, but a few. And for those precious little kids, it could literally be the difference between life and death.

The second thing that happens is that for the first time in the history of our country public schools were forced to compete for low income kids and the money those kids command. Parents and youngsters who had been ignored their entire lives suddenly were the focus of a very great deal of interest by the bureaucrats in the public schools. They saw that $2,500 walking out the door, and suddenly they took note. They sent surveyors around

> *For the first time in the history of our country, public schools were forced to compete for low income kids and the money those kids command. Parents and youngsters who had been ignored their entire lives suddenly were the focus of a very great deal of interest by the bureaucrats in the public schools. They saw that $2,500 walking out the door, and suddenly they took note.*

> *But the amazing thing is that over 50 percent of the public school teachers in Milwaukee send their children to private schools... These unions argue that if we take these kids out of the public schools, the public schools are going to fail. My solution is let the poor kids leave and let the bureaucrats send their kids to these schools.*
>
> *No one ever takes me up on that invitation.*

to low-income neighborhoods to ask: How can we keep you in our schools? How can we change?

Reform is being driven by competition even at this small level. But the public schools didn't stop with trying to improve. Of course they did what every good American would do, they went to court and filed a lawsuit.

They actually opened up a two-front battle against choice. The first was a lawsuit challenging the constitutionality of the choice program, and the second was that the state superintendent of public instruction, Bert Grover, unleashed a torrent of regulations designed to sentence this choice program to death by bureaucratic strangulation. That forced the parents to go to court to challenge those regulations as well. We had to win both of those court battles for choice to happen. We packed the courtroom with low-income parents, and the trial court judge ruled in our favor on both counts.

The choice program opened in 1990, and it was the dawn of a brand new day for kids who have never had a chance before. But the battle raged on in the courts, and the battle raged on in the court of public opinion as well.

I've learned a lot about guerrilla tactics from Polly Williams. She said, "You know, these teachers' unions have filed this lawsuit; they must really believe in the public schools." But the amazing thing is that over 50 percent of the public school teachers in Milwaukee send their children to private schools. Polly Williams said: "Okay. If these public schools are good enough for my kids, they're good enough for their kids. I am going to sponsor legislation that will require public teachers, as a condition of employment, to send their kids to public schools."

Guess what? This was not overwhelmingly supported. She received death threats on her telephone answering machine. It was really intense. She never did file that bill, fortunately. We would have had to challenge that one too. Even public school teachers have rights. The point was exactly made. These unions argue that if we take these kids out of the public schools, the public schools are going to fail. My solution is let the poor kids leave and let the bureaucrats send their kids to these schools. No one ever takes me up on that invitation.

We lost the battle in the Court of Appeals in Wisconsin and ultimately argued it in the Wisconsin Supreme Court. The Wisconsin Supreme Court by a 4 to 3 vote upheld the program in its entirety and embraced choice as a concept and as a potential solution to the crisis of inner city public education. I am very excited about that.

There were no federal issues in the lawsuit. So as far as this lawsuit is concerned, the lawsuit is successfully concluded and David has in fact slain Goliath.

There were a couple of lessons for me from the choice litigation.

One of the reasons I became a lawyer is that the playing field in the courtrooms is about as level a playing field as you can possibly find. The resources are still tremendously arrayed against low-income parents and advocates of choice, but everybody has the same number

of pages in their briefs, everybody has the same amount
of time to make their arguments, and since the arguments
are on our side legally, morally, economically, and politically, we will ultimately prevail. So I believe that litigation
must be a part of the arsenal.

If choice is successful in California, we already know
that it will be challenged in court. When Oregon sponsored
an initiative, we had agreed to represent it and, if it were
enacted, to defend it, because the parents have to be in the
courtroom. I paid a courtesy call on the local head of the
ACLU to see what her position was, and she said "Oh, we'll
be there. We'll be challenging it." And I said, "Do you
realize that you guys purport to be in favor of equal
education opportunities, and this would be the biggest
revolution that's ever taken place to deliver those educational opportunities to those who need them the most?"
And she said, "You don't understand, the moment one
dollar crosses the threshold into a religiously affiliated
school, that undoes the entire thing."

I think that is insane, and we will be there to defend
it. But we're going to take the offensive also. We plan to
file a series of test cases on behalf of low-income parents
challenging public school systems under state constitutional guarantees. Our theory in essence is a warranty
theory. If you bought a car and received a guarantee for
it, and your car turned out to be an utter lemon, you would
go to court. The court would not take over the car company.
It wouldn't order tax increases. It wouldn't put you on a
bus. It would give you your money back.

Likewise, in the educational context, the state requires you to go to school, it extracts money from you for
that purpose, and in return it guarantees a minimal—and
I emphasize *minimal*—quality of education. In the inner
cities it does not remotely—not remotely—approach that
level of quality. So we will represent low-income parents
challenging these school systems, putting the school sys-

tem literally on trial, and demanding the only remedy on earth that will solve the problem for these people and that is their ability to gain control of their children's education.

I have met some incredible people in the battle for choice. Almost all of them are children. And at the Wisconsin Supreme Court last fall, we had a busload of 8th graders from Urban Day School, a beautiful little private day school in Milwaukee, come to Madison to hear the court argument. Unfortunately, the bus was late, and by the time they got there the court was already packed with people, most of them bureaucrats. The kids couldn't get into the courtroom. I kept looking over my shoulder to see where they were, and just as I was about to get up to begin my argument I looked back and against the glass doors in the back of the courtroom were dozens of kids with their noses pressed against the windows looking in at what was going on.

Just as I was about to get up to begin my argument, I looked back and against the glass doors in the back of the courtroom were dozens of kids with their noses pressed against the windows looking in at what was going on. What a metaphor for what has been going on. These little kids—always on the outside looking in.

What a metaphor for what has been going on. These little kids—always on the outside looking in. With a victory in Wisconsin, those children are on the inside now. With your help and support, they will never be on the outside again.

PROPOSITION 174 IS BAD NEWS FOR CHILDREN AND TAXPAYERS

NO

On November 2, Californians will vote on an issue that has the potential to destroy public education. That issue is whether private schools should be supported by taxpayer dollars and allowed to discriminate against some children. The California Teachers Association and its education colleagues are vehemently opposed to this initiative—Proposition 174.

First, the initiative takes money away from our public schools—more than $2.6 billion even if no students transfer to a voucher school. Our schools lose 10 percent of their funding—meaning fewer teachers, teachers' aides, security offi-

California Teachers Association

The California Teachers Association represents 250,000 public school teachers in the state of California.

This is the CTA's statement on Proposition 174, the California school voucher initiative before California voters in November 1993. Reprinted with permission of the CTA.

Proposition 174 allows private schools to discriminate against students on the basis of gender, religion, income, and mental and physical ability tests. Too many students will find themselves shut out of the private schools of their choice. In fact, Proposition 174 isn't choice for students. It isn't choice for parents. It's choice for the private schools.

cers—and more crowded classrooms.

Second, it exempts voucher schools from teaching and learning standards. Teachers do not have to be certified. They don't even have to have college degrees. What's more, anyone who recruits 25 students could qualify as a voucher "school" and receive taxpayer dollars.

Even radical religious sects or political causes could qualify. In fact, a self-described coven of witches in Contra Costa County has already announced it will form a school and collect vouchers if the initiative passes.

Proposition 174 also makes regulation of voucher schools virtually impossible. No teacher or course requirement—no requirement of any kind—can be imposed on voucher schools without a three-fourths vote of the California Legislature. Eleven senators could block any proposed accountability measures for voucher schools.

The initiative also invites waste and fraud. It removes billions of dollars from neighborhood schools and hands them to private schools with no public audits to show how the money is spent.

Finally, it allows private schools to discriminate

against students on the basis of gender, religion, income, and mental and physical ability tests. Too many students will find themselves shut out of the private schools of their choice. In fact, Proposition 174 isn't choice for students. It isn't choice for parents. It's choice for the private schools.

Also, the new entitlement program created by Proposition 174 and the bureaucracy created to manage it will create pressure for a major tax increase. Taxpayers will end up footing the bill for Proposition 174.

Finally, the school vouchers initiative will violate the First and Fourteenth amendments to the U.S. Constitution. Legislative Counsel Bion M. Gregory of the California State Legislature has issued an opinion that Proposition 174 violates the Establishment clause of the First Amendment because it would make public funds available for sectarian private schools. There are sure to be court challenges of this initiative. It is altogether likely that a court might rule that religious schools are excluded from receiving vouchers, but private voucher schools can accept them.

Gregory notes that the money will flow directly from the state to religious schools. As a result, "the measure will have a beneficial effect as to religious institutions that is

The public schools are threatened by this voucher initiative. Can our public schools be improved? Of course they can. We want improvement, and it has been happening. But Proposition 174 does not improve public schools. It does not increase parental involvement, improve discipline, or reduce class size.

not merely indirect and incidental, but would subsidize and advance the religious mission of sectarian schools in violation of the First Amendment."

Gregory's report also states that the school voucher initiative will violate the Equal Protection Clause of the Fourteenth Amendment because it allows gender-based discrimination.

Public education has been a cornerstone of this nation for more than a century. The public schools are threatened by this voucher initiative. Can our public schools be improved? Of course they can. We want improvement, and it has been happening. But Proposition 174 does not improve public schools. It does not increase parental involvement, improve discipline, or reduce class size. And it hits at the heart of the democratic system that has made our country great.

Proposition 174 will do nothing to improve education or the public schools. Protect our future and the future of our children. Vote NO on Proposition 174.

EDUCATION REFORM THROUGH CHOICE

YES

A third key education reform is parental choice—full, unfettered choice over which schools their children will attend. In a free market economy, those who produce goods and services are ultimately answerable to the consumer; if the quality is shoddy, the consumer will buy someone else's product. It doesn't work that way in public education, though. Even when armed with adequate information about school quality (which they rarely have), parents in most places around the country are not permitted to transfer their children from a bad school to a good one.

In a sharp break with my predecessor, Terrel H.

William Bennett

William Bennett was Secretary of Education during the Reagan administration.

This material is adapted from William Bennett's book, *The Devaluing of America* (Summit Books, 1992), and is reprinted with permission of the author.

All parents, regardless of income, should be able to choose places where they know their children will learn. And they should be able to choose environments where their own values will be extended instead of lost.

Bell, I immediately voiced strong support for vouchers and tuition tax credits when I became Secretary of Education. "The idea of choice is an idea whose time has come," I said at a news conference announcing our proposal. The proposal urged that the federal Chapter 1 program (compensatory education for the disadvantaged) be administered through vouchers (averaging $600 each) in order to give students from less fortunate environments the chance to choose private schools, too. As I told the National Catholic Educational Association in 1985:

"All parents, regardless of income, should be able to choose places where they know their children will learn.

"And they should be able to choose environments where their own values will be extended instead of lost. It's possible that there are some public schools nobody would choose. They are so bad that they might suddenly find themselves without any students. But I have no idea why we should be interested in protecting schools like that from competition —or any schools from competition. Our worst schools are non-competitive schools, and that's no coincidence."

The philosophy behind the choice proposal is that we need to break the monopoly currently exercised by the state-run schools and allow all schools—including private and religious schools—to compete for public dollars. A full-scale voucher program would promote a healthy rivalry between public and private schools, as well as among public schools. Teachers' unions and the education establishment adamantly and uniformly oppose our voucher program, calling it "ridiculous" (Council of Great City Schools), "a Trojan horse," (National School Board Association), "offensive" (National Parent-Teacher Association), "a sham" (NEA), and a proposal that amounted to "cannibalization" (AFT).

The education establishment recognized our proposal for what it was; a direct and open challenge to their monopoly control of American education. The teachers' unions knew that if they lost on this issue of choice, their iron lock on power would be loosened. This is why full-scale choice was, and remains, the linchpin of sound educational reform.

The education establishment recognized our proposal for what it was; a direct and open challenge to their monopoly control of American education. The teachers' unions knew that if they lost on this issue of choice, their iron lock on power would be loosened. This is why full-scale choice was, and remains, the linchpin of sound educational reform.

Critics of full choice for American parents in the selection of schools argue that choice isn't right; public money should only go to public and not religious schools, and so full choice would amount to a violation of the separation of church and state. They have it wrong. Voucher bills have been proposed, including the one we advanced to Congress in 1986, that are fully constitutional. Most of our critics concede it to be so. Public money goes to Catholic and Jewish hospitals to care for the public, and public money supports fire and police forces that serve religious institutions. Public money should be for the education of the public, and a child in Catholic, Methodist, or Jewish school is every bit as much a member of the public as a child in a state-supported school.

There is another issue associated with choice as well—social justice. At present, our most affluent families do exercise choice, by buying a home in the neighborhood of their choice, or by sending their children to a private school. The poor do not now have that kind of choice. In contrast to the dismal report of the Chicago public schools, Chicago's Catholic schools are graduating 85 percent of their children at a cost of about $2,500 a year and with a fraction of the administrators per student (only 32 central-office administrators for more than 160,000 students). Since many Chicago public school teachers, knowing the relative strengths, choose private schools for their children, shouldn't others be given the same choice? It is a question of social justice.

The critics of elementary and secondary education school choice should also acknowledge the inconsistency and even hypocrisy of their position. The fact is, we already have a system of choice in American higher education and people don't object to it. When we give out billions of dollars every year for students to go to college, with their Pell grants or their Stanford loans, they can take them to Indiana University, Notre Dame, Yeshiva, or Liberty Baptist. Indiana University isn't diminished because Notre Dame is a fine school; Liberty Baptist isn't daunted because Notre Dame is a fine school. Broad choice in higher education hasn't hurt public higher education; on the contrary, greater competition has helped it and helped students. Why, then, do we not allow it at the elementary and secondary levels, which are so much more important and formative?

There is an additional benefit to choice. If we invite parents to choose their schools, it can be a good first step in the critical effort of reenfranchising them. Choice among schools is a first involvement in the schools, a critical investment, and it may lead to further involvement, which is something teachers long for. If parents know the results by school of tests with national standards, they will choose more wisely. The more we can do to involve (or reinvolve) parents, the better.

Choice advocates have some remarkably convincing

Broad choice in higher education hasn't hurt public higher education; on the contrary, greater competition has helped it and helped students. Why, then, do we not allow it at the elementary and secondary levels, which are so much more important and formative?

success stories to which they can point. One of the best is in the public system in local District 4 in New York's East Harlem. In the early 1970s, District 4 was an educational basket case. It ranked last in reading scores among all the city's 32 school districts. Then, under the leadership of superintendent Anthony Alvarado, the district allowed parents to choose for their children from a wide variety of newly restructured schools, each offering a particular instructional focus. In some instances, several minischools were created within the same building. Before the choice program began, only 15 percent of the students in the district could read at grade level. Recent test scores show 64 percent at or above grade level in reading and 53

> *"The quickest, surest way to explode the bureaucratic blob, escape from the self-seeking union and develop schools that succeed for children is to set up a voucher system."*

percent at or above grade level in math. According to William C. Myers of the Free Congress Foundation, the number of students from the district who qualified for admission to one of New York's prestigious specialized high schools increased from ten to 300, and today 96 percent of East Harlem graduates are admitted to college.

Today, East Harlem's teachers are energized and motivated. Lynne Kearney, director of District 4's Manhattan East School, says why: "People are here because they want to be ... There's a camaraderie, because this place doesn't have to exist. We can go out of business tomorrow. If it didn't meet needs, it would fold." According to a *New York Times* special report on the East Harlem school district, choice has "helped send test scores, teacher morale, and parent involvement soaring."

At the end of the great Chicago school debate, the *Chicago Tribune* argued for full choice: "The quickest, surest way to explode the bureaucratic blob, escape from the self-seeking union and develop schools that succeed for children is to set up a voucher system. That would bring new people into school management, assure local control, empower parents, squeeze out bad schools, and put the forces of competition to work for improving education."

MYTHS, MARKETS, AND SCHOOLS

John Mockler

John Mockler is a senior partner in Mockler Halnan Strategic Education Services, Inc. His clients include a large number of public school interests.

Adapted from the conference proceedings of "Rebuilding California's Schools, The Educational Choice Debate," May 1, 1992, San Francisco, CA, sponsored by the Pacific Research Institute.

L istening to people speak on this topic, I've been struck by the fervor and commitment to this concept of market forces in general, in government and, in particular, in public schools. It's almost a religious discussion.

Mythology is a powerful motivator. Anything you say about a system of public education in America or in the state is true, because somewhere in America there is evil in the public schools, and even in the private schools. But there is also goodness. So anything you say is true. And remember, on average, half of all students are always below the average.

> *Mythology is a powerful motivator. Anything you say about a system of public education in America or in the state is true, because somewhere in America there is evil in the public schools, and even in the private schools. But there is also goodness.*

I hear things like the "grade 12 norm." Do you know the difference between an 8th grade reading level and a 12th grade reading level on a grade 12 reading test? Three additional items correct on an 82-item test. Three items correct! All of this talk about achievement neglects these psychometric facts. Those are the statistics. That's not a myth; that's fact.

It seems to me the question is: Will market forces have a positive overall impact on the education quality in this state or in this nation? I don't know the answer to that; I'm certainly an open-ended nonbeliever on the question. I'm not certain. I can guarantee you that a lot of things are going on in the public schools that are awful. But I can also tell you a lot of things are good. Will market forces alter that? Maybe.

Joe Alibrandi's speech was wonderful. He has the passion, and this man has worked in the vineyards. The trouble is that when the question was SBA813 and when the question was restructuring I heard Joe give the same speech. He just plugged in this bill or that bill, and now it's going to be market forces in education. Well, maybe it works and maybe it doesn't. I'm not instinctively against market forces. We'll see in Milwaukee whether those kids get a better education. And if they do, we had best take that information and move it forward.

We may well see something about charter schools out of Minnesota. Analytically, I don't know whether it will work. There certainly was no real freedom of public or private choice in the East Harlem experiment. It was a great thing that went on—all inside the public schools. It cost tons of money, and they are doing a good job—but there was no private choice.

I'm not instinctively against market forces. We'll see in Milwaukee whether those kids get a better education. And if they do, we had best take that information and move it forward.

Having said all that, does this so-called initiative that has qualified for the California ballot in November provide choice in a context that is reasonably expected to improve education?

Now we have a real issue, and we need to intellectually analyze this initiative. Does it give parents choice? No, it does not! It allows any school to exclude any kid that it chooses to exclude. So parents do not have a choice. You only have a choice if that school will take your kid. And if that school will take the kid for the amount of the voucher or that plus some money you might add to it, that is not parental choice. That is a subsidy to certain private schools, which might be good or might not be, but let's not call it choice.

Is there any accountability? No. It is interesting that in this initiative every place they want to make sure something happens they say "you shall" or "shall not." And every level of accountability they say "may." They may if they choose have an accountability test but only—and this is in the Constitution in the State of California—only if it

61

> These technical mistakes in the constitution are not fixable. Nothing in this initiative can be fixed except with another constitutional amendment passed by the people.
> My favorite story of the Supreme Court ruling on intent is that if you intended it you should have written it that way in the first place.

meets or reflects national standards. National Standards! Guess what? There are no national standards!

Can you exclude certain kids? Well, you can't discriminate on the basis of race, ethnicity, color, or national origin if you want to take students with scholarships. But can you exclude by religion? Yes! Can you exclude by handicapping conditions? Yes! Can you exclude by "I just don't like you?" Yes! Analytically, that bothers me, maybe that doesn't bother you.

We know there are about 550,000 to 600,000 kids going to private schools now. Some are doing well; some are not. We know we are going to give the school at least $2,500 per child. So the public is going to spend a tax amount of $5 billion. How do we know that? The constitutional amendment says that you subtract both the costs of the voucher ($2,500) and the "savings" ($2,500) from public school funds. It also says you subtract full funding for the student transferred to the private school.

$1.3 billion for vouchers,
$1.3 billion for "savings,"
$2.4 billion for subtracting students
= $5 billion.

These technical mistakes in the constitution are not

fixable. Nothing in this initiative can be fixed except with another constitutional amendment passed by the people.

My favorite story of the Supreme Court ruling on intent is that if you intended it you should have written it that way in the first place. Market forces might have a positive value if properly implemented in the public school system. Unthought out, anti-intellectual religious fervor may move the issue forward politically, but please have a little more analytical rationale and factual basis before you support radical changes in the public schools.

THE REAL ISSUE

YES

Let's assume that we just got off the Mayflower, and we are trying to decide how this country is going to be structured. We firmly believe in freedom, free enterprise, and the freedom of individuals to make a choice. We said, in terms of college education, we're going to have competition. We are going to have private institutions. We can have public institutions too, but people are going to have a choice as to where they go to school. In preschool we are going to do the same thing. In all areas of commerce people are going to have the opportunity to make a choice as to whose product and whose service they buy.

Joseph P. Alibrandi

Joseph P. Alibrandi is CEO of Whittaker Corporation and chairman of ExCEL (Excellence through Choice in Education League), sponsor of Proposition 174, the parental choice in education initiative.

Adapted from the conference proceedings of "Rebuilding California's Schools, The Educational Choice Debate," May 1, 1992, San Francisco, CA, sponsored by the Pacific Research Institute.

> *It's ironic to feel that we, who want to change to what is really the main thrust of what makes this country great, are the people on the defensive, while those who want to support a system that is really an anachronism with regard to the rest of our society are on the offensive side of the issue.*

However, somebody in the back of the room says, wait a minute, on education—kindergarten through 12th grade—let's have that run by the government as a government monopoly. How would we react? We would all scream and holler and say that's ridiculous. That's totally foreign to the concept of the kind of society we want to create. Yet, where do we find ourselves today?

We find ourselves in a position where we want to provide the same freedom of choice, the same freedom of opportunity for all kids to share in education. We are saying that there must be a government-sponsored, socialistic, top-down run system—a monopoly of the government. It's ironic to feel that we, who want to change to what is really the main thrust of what makes this country great, are the people on the defensive, while those who want to support a system that is really an anachronism with regard to the rest of our society are on the offensive side of the issue. We are going to have to get down to fundamentals, and we're going to have to talk about what choice really means and the kind and quality of education that our kids are getting, or are not getting, these days.

I want to talk about the real issue in the State of California, and what I say about California I think applies to the rest of the country. In California, we have 5 million kids in our public school system. Of those 5 million, if we keep doing things the way we're doing them, 30 percent will drop out. That is in spite of all the programs to try to keep kids in school and to reduce the dropout rate—not by educating them better but by trying to find ways of keeping them there even though they are not constructively learning.

Thirty percent, or a million and a half kids, are going to drop out of school. Another 2 million will graduate at a 7th to 8th grade reading level, which means they will parade across the stage at graduation day and will be handed a diploma that most of them probably can't read. Now, this is what our educational system is producing today. And I, as a businessman, along with a lot of other business people—people in the California Business Roundtable, very well meaning, very dedicated people— have recognized this problem for many, many years.

It doesn't take a lot of talent to recognize it when you have applicants coming in for jobs who can't even fill out the application. At Pacific Bell, more than 60 percent of the high school graduates who applied for entry level jobs as telephone operators and telephone service people flunked a 7th to 8th grade reading test. That is pretty sad.

The world economy is demanding a work force with much higher skill levels. As a country able to compete in the world, we are sinking rather than gaining. The latest IEA studies showed tests of 10-year-olds and 14-year-olds in a lot of countries in the world. The most compelling thing to me in that study was that in the ten years between 1974 and 1984 every country in the world showed a massive improvement in the children's educational level in science and math—except the United States. The United States clearly and obviously stood out, because it was the only one where the line went down. And we are now at the

> *The fact that kids are coming out of the system unable to read doesn't enter into the equation. You don't see schools close down; you don't see people get fired.*

bottom behind Thailand in the level of education our kids are getting in science and math.

We are never going to be able to compete in a world scene with that caliber and quality of people. It used to be that you had your resources in the ground, and we had a lot of coal, oil, limestone, and ore. We had a competitive advantage in the world markets. That is not the case anymore. The one overwhelming advantage that a country has today is the quality of its intellectual capital. And ours is going in the wrong direction.

What happened to us? Why is it, and what are we going to do about it? Clearly the trend and quality of education keeps sinking.

I feel bad that it took us so long to realize that the problem is not the recipe; it's not whose recipe you use for managing schools. It doesn't matter whether it's Joe Alibrandi's or Milton Friedman's or somebody else's.

Let's suppose that the government decided 50 years ago that IBM, being the strongest, best capitalized company in the computer business, was going to be the computer business for the United States. Do you think we would have the computers we have today? Look at what happened over the last 50 years because of competition. Apple Computer has opened up a whole new market in personal computers. IBM has responded by not only trying to match their effort but to do better. And while they were doing that, two guys in Palo Alto, Bill Hewlett and Dave Packard, started the Hewlett Packard company in the area of scientific computers and again started taking a market share from IBM. And IBM had to react dramatically to not only match that effort but to do them one better. And while they were doing that, Decker on the East Coast started up with business computers doing exactly the same thing.

Now, if we had made that decision 50 years ago that IBM is the computer company for the United States, we would have computers today but there is no question in anybody's mind that we would not have benefited from the innovation and creativity that these other companies put forth in advancing the state of that art. And that updraft, if you will, that constant adaptation to the requirement and that constant updraft to improve is what is missing in the present school system.

Our education system is a monolithic monopoly, rule driven and not based on outcome. Teachers' requirements are to make sure you fill out all the forms. If you were to ask somebody on the school board "How are you doing?" they would say, "Great, we are doing just perfect because the teachers get all their forms in on time."

The fact that kids are coming out of the system unable to read doesn't enter into the equation. You don't see schools close down; you don't see people get fired. As a matter of fact, their is a listing of temporary advisers that we tried to find. These are really people who failed as principals or in other functions. With tenure, you can't fire them, so they get promoted to advisers. I ask the teachers' union, "Why do you use them as advisers?" They responded, "If we are going to try something new in a school system, we ask these advisers how they feel about it because they were principals."

Why not ask the guys who are succeeding instead of the guy who failed whether the system will work? That stifling concept—the inability to adapt to the needs of the community and this feeling that one system meets all

We've got to change the mentality so that the issue of public education is not that we as taxpayers made some commitment carved in stone to preserve this "institution" no matter what. Remember, our commitment is to educate all kids—the poor kids in the inner city just as well as the kids who live in Santa Barbara and other places around the state.

requirements—is a basic fallacy. We need to create that competitive updraft so schools are constantly trying to meet and improve on the requirements of their customers. We've got to change the mentality so that the issue of public education is not that we as taxpayers made some commitment carved in stone to preserve this "institution" no matter what. Remember, our commitment is to educate all kids—the poor kids in the inner city just as well as the kids who live in Santa Barbara and other places around the state.

We should all learn from a public school in Corona called the Lincoln Alternative School. The reason they call it "alternative" is because they teach things like math, physics, chemistry, and science. This school has really been a pioneer in a sense. The principal got together with his staff and said, "Look, we don't need clowns like Alibrandi telling us how to run schools, we know what it takes to run a school, and so we are going to find a way to break the rules and run the school in the way we think it ought to be run."

They called in the parents, and they said, "We would like to have a contract with each parent. You must attend a meeting of the school at least every two weeks. If you don't have a car, we will arrange for somebody to pick you up. If you don't have the time, we will adjust times. But you must meet the people of the school on a one-to-one basis at least once every two weeks." And in that contract they had dress codes for kids. Then they sat down with the teachers and had exactly the same kind of agreement with the teachers, including a dress code for teachers. And they laid out the whole format of what was going to be taught, and how people were going to be evaluated.

They felt concepts like busing were very impersonal. Their job was not only to educate kids but also to build community spirit. And so they said, "We'll get rid of buses. We are going to set up car pooling arrangements. And we want to have people beginning to worry about their neighbor's child, and try and build a community."

The long and the short of it is that in five years the scores of that school and the performance of that school have been fantastic by any measure. This is clearly a massive improvement.

So, obviously, as you would expect, people are climbing all over each other trying to figure out how to get their kids into that school. The school takes the kids who were normally allocated to that school and then open additional capacity on a first-come, first-served basis.

My nephew and his wife wanted their little boy Michael to get into that school. One day while my nephew was at work his wife called him and said: "Andy, I just drove by that school, and there are fathers with sleeping bags sleeping in the playground and forming a line to be there for the first-come, first-served enrollment, which begins at 8:00 AM on Thursday morning." (This is Tuesday afternoon.) So Andy went home, got his sleeping bag, and slept in that playground Tuesday night and Wednesday night and now Michael is at that school.

You look at that and say he got in and that's great.

But as a businessman my reaction is a little different. Suppose I were in my office and looked out the window and my competitor across the street had people sleeping in his parking lot for two days to buy his goods. My reaction would be to get my people together and say, "Hey guys, let's find out what he's doing, because we have to do one better than that. We absolutely have to do better than that, or we are out of business."

How did the schools in the neighborhood of the Lincoln Alternative react? They wrote letters to the district saying that the parents and the car pooling were blocking traffic at inappropriate times of the day. The school was breaking the rules. The same basic kind of harassment that Polly Williams got in Wisconsin.

That is the problem with the system. Instead of reacting in a way that a free enterprise business would react—looking at what they've done and saying that's a great innovation, how can we do better?—they fight that system.

What I hope to accomplish with Proposition 174 is not to move a lot of kids out of the public schools and into private schools. Frankly, I would consider that a failure, if that's what we do. What I want to do is put those parents in the adjoining schools in a position where they can go to the principal of their school and say: "Look, I don't want to take my child out of your school. But Lincoln Alternative is doing these things. We would like to understand why you don't do it? And if you don't do it, then we have the power to do something about it." Whereas today, those parents have no power to do anything about it at all.

That is the crux of what Proposition 174 is going to do. And I truly believe that this is going to do more to improve the public schools than any other reform effort ever tried.

The thing that probably concerns me most are statements that this will destroy the public schools, and that we shouldn't use tax money to put kids in private school. The reality is that the State of California is committed to providing kids with an education and not with preserving some institution. We are paying taxes to get our kids educated, not to maintain some institution that is failing to accomplish that. And when you really think about it, in the State of California you've got 5 million kids in the public schools, 500,000 in private schools—public schools have a 90 percent market share. Even if you have a great increase in private schools, public schools will still have an 85 percent market share.

Why does this massive monolithic organization fear giving parents the choice to choose their schools? Why this fear? This massive organization is spending $28 billion a year, has 90 percent of the market, and they fear giving parents the opportunity to choose where their kids go to school. What they are really saying is that unless they keep the kids incarcerated in their schools under the force of law they can't function. If their customers have freedom, they can't function. I find that appalling.

Now, if somebody said to me that in my business I could have 90 percent market share and my competitor could only get half the price for his product that I get for mine, and if I were to worry about that sort of competition,

> *Why does this massive monolithic organization fear giving parents the choice to choose their schools? Why this fear? This massive organization is spending $28 billion a year, has 90 percent of the market, and they fear giving parents the opportunity to choose where their kids go to school.*

> *With the tremendous competitive advantage public schools have ... if people are concerned this is going to cause a major shift of kids out of the public schools and into the private schools, that purely and simply underscores the fact that we have a very serious problem, and we've got to deal with it.*

I've got a real problem. That is the issue. With the tremendous competitive advantage public schools have, and with the fact that the other schools are going to operate at half the cost, if people are concerned this is going to cause a major shift of kids out of the public schools and into the private schools, that purely and simply underscores the fact that we have a very serious problem, and we've got to deal with it.

I think Proposition 174 is going to do more to improve the public schools than any restructuring or choice legislation you are going to see. You are going to see choice legislation coming out of Sacramento. I happen to believe that a lot of that is just a backfire to Proposition 174. I'm sure the establishment would like to have a lot of people feel that choice legislation was passed, therefore we don't need Proposition 174. Please don't be fooled. For a choice system to work, it ought to be what we deserve—a full, complete and free choice system.

We can't afford not to have Proposition 174. It's okay if the Post Office delivers my letters three days late. I can live with that. But to destroy the opportunity for a lot of kids who are coming along behind us is a price we cannot afford to pay.

VOUCHERS: NOT IN THE PUBLIC INTEREST

NO

Ralph Flynn

Ralph Flynn, a former teacher in Boston, is executive director of the California Teachers Association (CTA), a 235,000 member affiliate of the NEA.

You don't have to be a social democrat or a democratic socialist, and I'm neither, to recognize that there are some services that are not only legitimate but necessary for government to provide. The American people decided a long time ago that free universal public education was one of those services. Public schools have served our nation well. I maintain they continue to serve our nation well, for all that their failures are far better advertised than their achievements.

That aside, should parents have educational choice? I suspect that every one of the California Teachers Association's 235,000 mem-

Adapted from the conference proceedings of "Rebuilding California's Schools, The Educational Choice Debate," May 1, 1992, San Francisco, CA, sponsored by the Pacific Research Institute.

> Parents should have the right to send their children to any private school, whether it's religious or secular. What we object to is the notion that taxpayer dollars should subsidize that choice.

bers would answer "yes." Parents should have the right to send their children to any private school, whether it's religious or secular. What we object to is the notion that taxpayer dollars should subsidize that choice. There are, in fact, a number of private school advocates who agree with us and believe the old adage that if you take the king's shilling you become the king's man. Some private schools will refuse the opportunity to participate in public funding. But let's face it, their number will be minuscule.

Now some of Dr. Milton Friedman's most earnest disciples also agree with us, at least in part, but for very different reasons. They support choice, or vouchers, because they see it as the thin edge of the wedge—an opportunity to introduce what Myron Lieberman calls "load shedding." Inherent in the concept of load shedding is a belief that taxes should not support any kind of education, private or public, which leads to the ultimate conclusion that the really true free marketeer is a closet anarchist.

The diversion of public funds to private and church-run institutions is at the center of the debate in California about the voucher initiative sponsored by Mr. Joseph Alibrandi. The California Teachers Association led the campaign to prevent that initiative from qualifying. And the California Teachers Association will do whatever it can to defeat that initiative at the polls when it is on the ballot in November. We will do everything possible to defeat this initiative because we believe it will financially devastate the California public schools.

The analysis provided by the California Department of Education of the impact of this proposed constitutional change on March 5th of this year states: "Should a student transfer to a private school from a public school, the school would lose $5,200 that is now spent to educate it." In addition, however, half that amount, or $2,600—that's an additional $2,600—would revert from the education budget to the General Fund of the state. Another $2,600 would be removed from the guarantee to fund public education that now exists under Proposition 98. In other words, we would lose twice as much as we are now spending to educate a child in the public school. The effect overall would be that all public schools would be hurt.

The California Teachers Association will do whatever it can to defeat that initiative at the polls when it is on the ballot in November.

If only 10 percent of the currently enrolled students transferred out of public to private schools, we would lose 20 percent of our total public school funding. That is a formula to destroy public schools—even though that may not be the intent.

Ironically, some of those who would be most at risk, should this initiative pass, are the advocates of parochial and other religious schools. If the California Supreme Court or the United States Supreme Court were to throw out the provisions of the initiative that give them taxpayer dollars, one of two things would happen. Either they would have to divorce themselves from their sponsoring churches, thus totally undermining their reason for exist-

I suggest to you that offers of choice programs in this particular initiative are an even more radical change in our schools than mandatory busing ever was.

ence, or they alone among nonpublic schools would be denied public monies, which would doom most of them to extinction.

But beyond that is a fact that dominates California's classrooms today. That fact is our state's enormous demographic diversity. Most of you, I suspect, know that 87 percent of the children in Los Angeles are ethnic and racial minorities. That number has dulled our senses. But think about this. In all the other school districts in California, the percentage of minority students is already above 44 percent and is rising rapidly.

In his book, *Free to Choose,* Dr. Friedman says, "We have always been proud and with good reason of the role that public schooling has played in fostering the assimilation of newcomers into our society, preventing fragmentation and enabling people from different cultural and religious background to live together in harmony." He then goes on to say, "Unfortunately, in recent years this reputation has become tarnished." And I agree. This system is on overload. How can we expect to build an interdependent civil society if one of the primary socializing institutions of our society, the public school, is balkanized or even worse.

In the 1960s, conservative critics assailed the so-called social engineers. Those of us, and I was one of them, who advocated the Great Society were criticized for trying to institute radical change in our schools through the use of mandatory busing. Now those of us who supported that radical change were aware of, but underestimated, the cost attendant on that change. We learned one of the hard lessons taught by the law of unintended effects. It manifested itself, in part, in white flight.

The message I'm getting from the teachers, as their employee, is that they do not believe that this proposition is in their interest.

Radical change of fundamental systems in any society is very dangerous business. I suggest to you that the voucher program in this particular initiative is an even more radical change in our schools than mandatory busing ever was. Think hard about the law of unintended effects, because typically it does not make itself evident until after the fact. Our public schools have their flaws, there is no question about it. What institution doesn't, including the medical delivery system? This proposition, however, could have the unintended effect of undermining what is good in our schools without at all touching what is wrong with our schools. What we could do with this initiative is hit the nail right on the thumb.

Where are the teachers? I'm an employee and not an officer of the CTA, and I serve at the pleasure of a board of directors of full-time teachers. The day I stop representing their interests is the day they find someone else to do it. The message I'm getting from them, as their employee, is that they do not believe that this proposition is in their interest.

1

DOES THE NEA SUPPORT CHOICE?

The National Education Association (NEA) supports a variety of choice options within the public schools—alternative programs such as magnet schools attracting students from throughout a school district, programs for students with special learning needs, and other options within school districts, in particular those developed in tandem with comprehensive school improvement plans. This support does not extend to public school choice plans that are federally or state-mandated, such as so-called interdistrict or open enrollment systems, since there is virtually no evidence that such plans im-

National Education Association

The NEA represents 2.1 million educators nationwide and is the largest and most powerful union in the U.S. today.

This material is drawn from the NEA's publication, "School Choice: Questions and Answers," and is reprinted with permission.

The National Education Association (NEA) supports a variety of choice options within the public schools... This support does not extend to public school choice plans that are federally or state-mandated, such as so-called interdistrict or open enrollment systems, since there is virtually no evidence that such plans improve educational quality or achievement.

prove educational quality or achievement.

The NEA remains unalterably opposed to any mechanism promoting the kinds of choice—such as tax credits or tuition vouchers—that would transfer public funds to private schools. Diverting public monies to private schools—schools that are selective in their entrance requirements, serve a strictly private purpose, and are accountable to no one but themselves—will do nothing to upgrade and enhance public education, the system responsible for educating the vast majority of our nation's students.

NEA Criteria for Judging Choice/Parental Options Plans

To aid NEA affiliates and public policymakers in judging the efficacy, quality, and equity of education provided under choice or parental option plans, NEA has developed a list of criteria, which follows:

1) Every choice plan should state its purpose and intended outcomes at the outset.

2) The plan should be designed primarily to improve the quality of instructional and educational programs in the public schools.

3) The plan should promote equal educational opportunity for all students, and should operate in ways that facilitate better racial, ethnic, and socioeconomic balances in the public schools.

4) The plan should be legal, constitutional, and in full compliance with court decisions and with federal, state, and local mandates.

5) The plan should provide adequate resources to ensure quality education programs for every student.

6) The plan should strengthen decentralization and local control, as well as public accountability over the schools.

7) The plan should in no way lead to the privatization of the public schools.

8) The plan should be consistent with and support existing collective bargaining procedures between school personnel and school governance, and should safeguard teacher transfer and other contractual or constitutional rights.

9) The plan should not impose additional administrative burdens on the teaching staff or additional regulatory requirements for school districts.

10) The plan should strengthen collaborative and cooperative efforts within and among schools.

Diverting public monies to private schools—schools that are selective in their entrance requirements, serve a strictly private purpose, and are accountable to no one but themselves—will do nothing to upgrade and enhance public education, the system responsible for educating the vast majority of our nation's students.

11) The plan should be based on the needs and input of students, parents, the school staff, and the community at large.

12) The plan must address access to transportation for all students.

13) The plan should provide the resources and information necessary to ensure that every parent understands and is able to gain access to the choices available.

14) The plan should include measures that truly empower parents, educators, and others in the community in the quest for improved community-based schools.

15) The plan should carefully spell out the roles and responsibilities of governmental officials, parents, educators, and the community in the development, implementation, and evaluation of any program.

CAN EDUCATION REFORM EDUCATION?

Wilbert Smith

Wilbert Smith is a former member of the Pasadena Unified School District Board of Education.

I don't believe we are talking about an initiative that is designed to promote private schools but more an initiative that is designed to improve public education. Let me tell you what is happening in my school district.

You see I am on the front line. I was a member of the board of trustees for the Pasadena Unified School District. For the last four years I did everything I possibly could to promote a discussion of educational reform because I thought that was only rational. In fact, I campaigned vigorously for my assignment on the school board and had a number of things I wanted to put in place. It never

Adapted from the conference proceedings of "Rebuilding California's Schools, The Educational Choice Debate," May 1, 1992, San Francisco, CA, sponsored by the Pacific Research Institute.

85

> I campaigned vigorously for my assignment on the school board and had a number of things I wanted to put in place. It never dawned on me that I would not be able to convince my fellow board members that if we continue to do what we have always done, we are going to continue to get what we already have.

dawned on me that I would not be able to convince my fellow board members that if we continue to do what we have always done, we are going to continue to get what we already have.

In the Pasadena Unified School District we run about $125 million a year through the turnstiles. And the people in my community who head that process are people who have limited expertise in management and business. This community did not ask the right questions before only a small portion of our 108,000 eligible voters went to the polls—even decided that public education was important enough to vote on. So we got what we deserved.

If you were running a private corporation and your gross revenue was $125 million a year, I guarantee you that even I would not be a member of your board of trustees or board of directors. If we think we can rely on education to change education, we have a rude awakening ahead of us.

We need to clearly understand what is ahead of us, and how this particular initiative is not only designed to improve public education but as well provide a significant savings over trying to educate these children in public institutions at $5,200 per child per year. In 1980, the census information reflected about 24 million people in the state of California. The census information in 1990 reflected 30 million people. As of 1990, we have some 5 million kids in our public educational system.

If we think we can rely on education to change education, we have a rude awakening ahead of us.

The finance department for the State of California—this is not some special interest group, this is the State of California—clearly states there is a projection of about a 40 percent increase in the number of kids that will soon come into our public school system. To house those kids we need about $30 billion—just to build infrastructure for these kids. The state legislature has set aside about $6 billion. That is a $24 billion shortfall. Where is it going to come from?

How much is $24 billion? Well, last year, if you recall, we had a $13 billion shortfall. To put it in perspective, if we closed the Department of Corrections for the entire State of California, and all the UC campuses in the state of California, and all the Cal-State universities in the state of California, we would save ourselves $10 billion. Now, purely from an economic standpoint, if we don't find some way to house some of these kids, we will be looking at 50 to 55 students per classroom. By the year 2000 we will be begging any institution that we can find to take some of these kids, because our constitution says that each one of them is guaranteed an education.

I don't think the issue we are tossing around today is one purely of more money. A *Los Angeles Times* article stated that to educate a child in a Catholic archdiocese costs about $1,700 per year. I went to a high school called Verbum Dei in the Los Angeles area, located in the heart

In my school district, 80 percent of our students are black or Hispanic. During the 1991/92 school year, the average grade was a "D." Hispanics performed at a 1.92 average and blacks at a 1.83 average. While there are some great programs addressing a limited few, we are not addressing the education of a vast number of kids we push out year after year.

of Watts. It is an all male school whose enrollment is 95 percent black and Hispanic. Of that 95 percent enrollment, 90 percent graduate, and 85 percent of them go on to college. And that is at an expense of $2,400 a year. Clearly what is happening there is that they believe in those kids; there is a process going on that says you can be somebody.

I've been to classrooms in my school district, and I'll see 90 percent Hispanic kids there, and I'll see a picture of George Washington on the wall or Abraham Lincoln. What about the self-esteem of these kids?

That Catholic archdiocese in Los Angeles county has 100,000 students. LA Unified School District has 810,000 students, including its day and evening instruction. The *Los Angeles Times* says that to manage those 810,000 students, there are 3,500 employees down at headquarters. The Catholic archdiocese, with one-eighth the population, should have 437 employees down at headquarters. But they don't. They manage 100,000 students with 25 employees. The *Los Angeles Times* reports that only one half of each educational dollar reaches the classroom. Perhaps this is partially explained when we consider that the Los Angeles Unified School District has 31 employees who earn salaries of more than $100,000 a year. There are not 31 employees in the entire Los Angeles County government making more than $100,000 a year. In the Los Angeles Unified School District 133 people make over $90,000; 607 over $80,000; 1,795 over $70,000; and 8,052 over $60,000. And 93 supposedly temporary consultants make $75,000 a year, with no job description. There can be no doubt why "educrats" with such a vested interest in maintaining the status quo are so vigorously opposed to a voucher initiative.

Some minorities are doing very well in private schools, and a number of minority groups are very excited about opening up private schools. If we continue to do what we've always done, we will continue to get what we already have. In my school district, 80 percent of our students are black or Hispanic. During the 1991/92 school year, the average grade was a "D." Hispanics performed at a 1.92 average and blacks at a 1.83 average. While there are some great programs addressing a limited few, we are not addressing the education of a vast number of kids we push out year after year.

THE CASE FOR CHOICE

YES

Milton Friedman

Milton Friedman, senior research fellow at the Hoover Institution and 1976 Nobel laureate, first proposed educational choice in a 1955 article included in his 1962 book Capitalism and Freedom *(with Rose Friedman).*

Adapted from the conference proceedings of "Rebuilding California's Schools, The Educational Choice Debate," May 1, 1992, San Francisco, CA, sponsored by the Pacific Research Institute.

It is a pleasure to be here with people all of whom I know are devoted to the same objective. Any differences among us are not with respect to objectives, and I think it is important to keep that in mind.

Whether we are in favor of or opposed to the voucher initiative, I am sure every one of us would like to see a world in which every youngster in the country has an opportunity to get schooling that will enable him or her to use his or her resources to the maximum possible benefit. Keep that in mind because we sometimes tend to think that this is a question between evil people and good people. It is

We are first class in higher education; we are third class in elementary and secondary schooling. Isn't that a paradox?

not. It is a question of method and not of objective.

I want to pose for you what seems to me like a paradox that illuminates like a spotlight why people like us—Joe Alibrandi, Sally Pipes, myself—are in favor of choice in education. Suppose you go around the world, any country you want to, and ask the following two questions. First, what country leads the world in higher education, in colleges and universities? Wherever you go around the world, you will get the same answer: the United States. We are the magnet for people from around the world who want to go to colleges and universities. At every one of our leading colleges and universities a significant fraction of students come from abroad. Some of them stay here, but most go back.

Now suppose you go around the world and ask exactly the same question about elementary and secondary schools. There will not be a single person around the world who will list the United States as a leader. We are first class in higher education; we are third class in elementary and secondary schooling. Isn't that a paradox? After all, the people who will become the students in our institutions of higher learning come from the elementary and secondary schools, and the people who teach in the elementary and secondary schools come from our institutions of higher learning.

What is the magic explanation? What is the answer? Why is it that we are world class on one level and third class on another level? For exactly the same reason that the Soviet Union is a disaster and the United States is an affluent country. At the higher level you have competition. There are government schools but there are also private schools.

Government schools, unfortunately from my point of view, have been gaining on private schools. Before World War II, roughly 50 percent of all students were in private schools in higher education; now only about one-fifth are. However, the important point is not that it is government or private, but that there are many alternatives among which the customers who are the students can choose.

There are 50 state universities as well as a great many private universities and colleges. Students from California can choose among a variety of different colleges and universities in California or they can choose colleges in other states. So you have competition, and no college or university can exist unless it attracts students.

There is no captive audience. It's not a fair game; it's not fair competition. It is the most unfair competition there is. If a youngster from the state of California wants to go to the University of California or one of the other state schools, he gets a free scholarship equivalent maybe to $5,000 or $10,000 a year. However, if he wants to go to let's say my old home base, the University of Chicago, not a penny for him. He doesn't get any scholarship from the state. It's a silly system; it's an unfair system. The government is offering something at half price as a subsidy but nonetheless, fair or unfair, it is a system in which there is competition among government institutions and private institutions. And we are world class.

Now consider the elementary and secondary level. The problem is not that bad people designed it. It is not that at all. As a good Marxist would say, it's the system.

At the elementary and secondary level you have a monopoly; you have a single organization. Of course, there are 50 different states, but youngsters at the elementary and secondary level do not have the freedom to choose

> *Some members of the educational establishment have been trying to co-opt the idea of choice by agreeing to choice but limiting it to government schools. I believe that would ultimately be the kiss of death for the choice idea and for improving the schools.*

among different states that they will have when they get older. They are pretty well committed to staying where their parents are. And there is a single monopoly that provides schooling in the state of California, a monopoly heavily centralized in Sacramento. Students have to go to the school to which they are assigned; they can't choose where to go.

I may say, as an aside, that some members of the educational establishment have been trying to co-opt the idea of choice by agreeing to choice but limiting it to government schools. I believe that would ultimately be the kiss of death for the choice idea and for improving the schools. A monopoly is a monopoly is a monopoly. A socialist institution is a socialist institution is a socialist institution, and the school system in the United States next to the military is by far and away the most socialized industry in the country with 90 percent of elementary and secondary students going to government schools and only 10 percent to private schools.

We use the words "public" and "private." I think that is a very misleading use of words. I do not see any respect whatsoever in which the university I am now associated with, Stanford, is in any sense less public than Berkeley or San Francisco State. They are all public institutions. The difference is not public; it is government versus nongovernment. Stanford is a nongovernment institution;

> *There is no respect whatsoever in which parents of children who are poor, who live in the slum areas or the low-income areas in the inner cities of Los Angeles, of San Francisco, of New york, of Chicago—there is no respect in which they are so disadvantaged as with respect to the kind of schooling they can get for their children.*

Berkeley is a government institution, and 90 percent of our students in the elementary and secondary schools are in government schools. Their parents have no choice.

There are some very good government schools. In general, where are they? In almost all cases they are in high-income neighborhoods. They are in the suburbs where a lot of high-income people are concentrated, people who are in a position to exercise control over their local schools.

I have argued repeatedly that those excellent schools in high-income districts ought to be regarded as tax shelters. If the people who live in those areas were to send their children to comparable private schools, the tuition they would pay would not be deductible in computing their income tax. However, if they have a private school in the guise of a so-called public school, the taxes they pay to support such schools are deductible in computing the federal income tax, and that is the sense in which they are tax shelters.

There are some very good schools in lower income neighborhoods as well. Yet there isn't the slightest doubt that we have in the United States what Assemblywoman Delaine Eastin warned us against having, namely a two-tiered educational system. There is no respect whatsoever in which parents of children who are poor, who live in the slum areas or the low-income areas in the inner cities of Los Angeles, of San Francisco, of New York, of Chicago—there is no respect in which they are so disadvantaged as with respect to the kind of schooling they can get for their children.

If they have the money, they can buy the same automobile anybody else can buy. If they have the money, they can buy the same foodstuffs anybody else can buy. However, even if they have the money, they cannot buy the same schooling. They are tied as captive customers to a monopoly school system.

I often use the analogy that if we give food stamps to people why don't we make them spend them in government grocery stores? What do you think those grocery stores would be like? Do you think they would match the supermarkets? Don't kid yourself.

The same force that explains the paradox between lower education and higher education explains why it is that when by a fluke United Parcel Service was able to go into competition with the Post Office in delivering packages, it took away all the Post Office's business. The same force explains why automobile manufacturers have no difficulty in manufacturing all the automobiles anybody wants to buy. If you want to buy an automobile, you won't find a shortage, but if you try to find a place to drive it you might. That is because highways are provided by the government and the cars are provided by private enterprise.

I hope Assemblywoman Eastin will pardon me if I take her as the butt of my comments. She referred to airline deregulation during the 1990s. I just ask you to consider what has happened in that area. People who were never before able to fly from one place to another have been able to fly. There has been a tremendous growth in traffic on the airlines. Who have benefited by airline deregulation? Low income people. Who have been harmed? High income people. You don't have the kind of exclusive possibility of service that you used to have when you had all fares fixed.

Take trucking. There has been an enormous increase in the availability of trucking and a great decline in the cost of trucking. Deregulation in those areas has had exactly the same kind of effects as deregulation would have in the area of schooling.

One more example. The airlines seem to be able to provide all the aircraft that people want to fly. Our deregulated airlines are losing money. That's a good thing. That shows that there is real competition, that they have to compete for customers. But again, where is the bottleneck? At the airports, in landing spaces, in gates? Why? The same reason: government monopoly. The engine of progress, growth, and development is competition.

Let me emphasize again that government versus private is an important element, but not the essential feature. If there is enough competition among government units, they too will have to shape up.

The deterioration in our school system is not a recent phenomenon. It really goes back 75 years. What produced it was largely a reduction in the number of school districts, and an accompanying centralization of control.

Terry Moe probably has a better number than I have, but my recollection is that there were well over 100,000 school districts early in this century. There are now 16,000. The producer rather than the consumer has been in the saddle, and the results are clear for all to see.

Now we come to the California initiative. How can we do anything about this problem? There is no way whatsoever of doing something about this problem except by introducing competition, by enabling customers, parents and children, to have alternatives among which they can choose.

We in the middle- and upper-income groups have had choice all along ... The poor suckers who live in Watts have no such alternative. Choice is what is necessary to give them that alternative. We want a system under which those poor parents will have at least something like the degree of freedom of choice that we now have for our children.

We in the middle- and upper-income groups have had choice all along. We can afford to pay twice for schooling—once through taxes and once through tuition, or we can afford to move to one of those high-income areas and take advantage of the tax shelters. The poor suckers who live in Watts have no such alternative. Choice is what is necessary to give them that alternative. We want a system under which those poor parents will have at least something like the degree of freedom of choice that we now have for our children.

This is something I have been associated with for 30 years, and I want to tell you briefly about my experience over that 30 years. I have repeatedly been involved in attempts to get choice and voucher initiatives, and repeatedly the same events have occurred. The public at first is in favor of it, but then the educational establishment gears itself up. It is able to outspend people who are in favor of choice, and it is able to destroy and beat down the attempt to get a voucher system adopted.

My first experience was over 20 years ago in New Hampshire where we used to have a second home. The head of the State Board of Education of New Hampshire at the time was William Bittenbender, a retired businessman who became very much interested in vouchers. Moreover, this was during the Nixon administration and its Office of Economic Opportunity had people who were interested in promoting choice in schooling.

So they provided financing for Mr. Bittenbender to have a study made in preparation for a model voucher plan for New Hampshire. He had some people at Dartmouth do a very good study. They devised a plan which was going to be done experimentally in five different cities in New Hampshire. All of those cities on first being approached agreed to participate in the plan.

> *The group that generally is most strongly in support are the blacks, who consistently give a 2 to 1 vote in favor of the voucher system.*

Then the educational establishment began to realize what was involved, and they went to work. Through their political clout, they ended up in each case getting the city to withdraw its agreement and nothing came of the effort. I have gone through the same experience in Connecticut and in Michigan. We have people here who can testify to the same experience in Oregon.

If you look at the way people vote when they are asked about choice in public opinion polls, a majority of the American people are in favor of choice in education, of a voucher system. The group that generally is most strongly in support are the blacks, who consistently give a 2 to 1 vote in favor of the voucher system.

On the other hand, suppose you look at the political scene. Rank-and-file blacks want a voucher system, but do their political leaders? Polly Williams is a great exception, the very first of the black leaders who really was willing to stand up for what was good for her constituents. People have mentioned that she was the chairwoman for Jesse Jackson in the state of Wisconsin.

I once had an occasion to ride in a private plane with Jesse Jackson from a meeting at which he and I had both spoken. They gave us a private plane to take us from that meeting somewhere in one of these wonderful places in the mountains near Washington to Washington, D.C. I used the occasion to talk to Jesse Jackson about the voucher system.

Rev. Jackson pretended that he had never heard of it—I think better of him than that. At any rate, I asked him where his children were going to school, and he did have one or two who were in public schools but a couple of others were in private schools. I explained the system and said why I thought that the people who would benefit from it most would be the blacks in the slum areas. He expressed great interest and said he was going to think about it.

Have you ever heard a word from him about it since? I haven't either. Why? Because a government monopolized school system is a source of political clout. Jesse Jackson was primarily in Chicago at that time. Where did he get his political clout in Chicago? He had something to say about who was on the school board, about who were the employees of the school board. He had patronage there. The black politicians who are willing to give up that political patronage for the benefit of their constituents are few and far between.

That is why it is so important to get this California initiative adopted. We never had a better chance than we have this year in my opinion. The anti-incumbent attitude on the part of the public at large, the increasing concern about the character of schooling, the awakening recognition by the business community that prospective future employees are not going to be schooled and that they are going to have to do the job over again—all of these things cooperate.

The one major obstacle, and it is a major obstacle, is the people whom Mr. Flynn represents. Not the teachers. Don't misunderstand me. I have over and over again talked to teachers in public schools who have been all in favor of the voucher system. It's the trade union leaders and the trade union bureaucrats, it's the people who occupy the positions in Sacramento and the educational bureaucracy, it's the Bill Honigs—those are the people who are the great opponents. That's our obstacle and it is a very real one.

Again, it is not because they are bad people. It's because there is one thing you can depend on everybody to do, and that is to put his interests above yours. That's what we are doing, and that's what they are doing. And they are right to be concerned.

If the voucher initiative is adopted, if we can get a competitive school system going, total cost of schooling will go down drastically, the amount of money available for paying their salaries will go down, but the quality of schooling available to children will go up.

There will be many more choices, there will be a whole rash of new schools that will come into existence. The government school system will improve, and the private school system will improve as someone correctly said this morning. So they are right to be concerned.

Their interest is in defeating this, but our interest is in assuring that it is passed. And I hope at least the business community in the state of California will wake up and not be shortsighted with respect to this issue as they have been on so many other occasions.

VOICES ON CHOICE

The Education Reform Debate

edited by

K. L. Billingsley

**Pacific Research Institute for Public Policy
San Francisco, CA**

Permission acknowledgments appear on page 102.

ISBN 0-936488-75-1

Printed in the United States of America
1   2   3   4   5   6   7   8   9   0

Pacific Research Institute for Public Policy
755 Sansome Street, Suite 450
San Francisco, CA 94111
(415) 989-0833

Director of Publications *Kay Mikel*
Cover Design *Lawrence Hernandez*
Printing and Binding *Haskin Press*

Library of Congress Cataloging-in-Publication Data
Voices on choice : the education reform debate / edited by K.L.
Billingsley.
p.   cm.
ISBN 0-936488-75-1
1. School choice—United States.   2. Educational vouchers—United
States.   3. Educational change—United States.   I. Billingsley,
Lloyd.
LB1027.9.V65   1994   93-36884
371'.01—dc20   CIP